The Anti-Inflammatory Cookbook

Autoimmune Protocol-Friendly Recipes from a Chef's Kitchen

Shannon Berends

Images by Alexis Berends Photography
Nutritional review by Zoe Schwartz, Registered Dietitian

www.mascotbooks.com

The Anti-Inflammatory Cookbook: Autoimmune Protocol-Friendly Recipes from a Chef's Kitchen

Photography by Alexis Berends, Alexis Berends Photography

Nutritional review by Zoe Schwartz, Registered Dietician, MS Nutrition

For more information, please contact:
Mascot Books
620 Herndon Parkway, Suite 320
Herndon, VA 20170
info@mascotbooks.com

Library of Congress Control Number: 2021909362

CPSIA Code: PREG0322A
ISBN-13: 978-1-64543-969-1

Printed in China

I want to dedicate this book to my amazing husband, my beautiful daughter, Nova, and my family. They have always given me the encouragement, love, and push to write this cookbook and research all these chef-inspired recipes. Thank you to the world's most handsome and willing taste tester, my amazing husband Richard. Thank you to my mom for always being there to listen to my worries about starting this project and reassuring me that I could make it happen; to my dad for constantly pushing me and believing in me and this project and being my biggest fan; to my sister for reading all of my recipes to ensure they were easy to understand, along with being my confidant and best friend; to my daughter, Nova, for changing my world in the best way possible and teaching me something new about life each day; to my mother-in-law for pushing me to publish this book; to my fluffy, smart cat, Melow, and my incredible, smart dog, Pluto.

INTRODUCTION

started my journey in baking and cooking with my grandmother when I was about six years old. My grandmom would always cook amazing spaghetti and meatball meals for my large Italian and Irish family every Sunday night. It was in those family moments that I realized that food has the potential to change someone's world. A person can go from having the worst day to enjoying a home-cooked meal with family and friends and end their day with laughter and smiles. Food brings us together and makes us whole.

I then decided that I wanted to devote my whole life to creating those special moments for and with other people. I worked at a local bakery, Weinrich's Bakery, in Willow Grove, Pennsylvania, in high school and during holidays throughout college. It was there that I met Stephen Weinrich, who taught me that running a bakery was not just about icing cakes, but also about incredible business skills, dedication, and determination. I was then inspired to go to The Culinary Institute of America, which as far as I'm concerned ,is Walt Disney World for chefs. I studied culinary science, along with baking and pastry arts. It was there that I learned the importance of understanding how ingredients interact. I also learned about specialty diets such as gluten-free, kosher, dairy-free, vegan, and more. I began to piece together my knowledge of food science and culinary baking arts to form one delicious universe.

After college I went on to work for a variety of different companies producing manufactured food and snack recipes. Amid all of my work, one experience that really stood out to me was becoming a personal chef for a local family whose son had an autoimmune disorder. I quickly realized there was a huge blank space in the market for anti-inflammatory and autoimmune friendly recipes that tasted as though a chef had created them.

I began remembering how important those dinners at my grandmom's house with family and friends were and thinking about how I never had to wonder if I could eat all the food on the table. It was then that I realized I wanted to create recipes that anyone with any inflammatory or autoimmune disorder could enjoy with family and friends who may not have those same dietary needs. I wanted to write recipes that tasted so good everyone would want to eat them. That is how I got started on this journey and how the *Anti-Inflammatory Cookbook* came about. I hope your family and friends enjoy these dishes as much as mine have. From my table to yours, bon appétit!

NOTE TO READERS

If you are on the elimination autoimmune diet, consult with your doctor prior to adding specific ingredients such as coconut sugar, maple syrup, honey, or spices to your recipes.

CONTENTS

1. Breakfast 1

2. Snacks 22

3. Meat 39

4. Seafood 63

5. Vegetables 80

6. Sauces, Dressings, Seasonings 112

7. Sides 154

8. Dessert 175

TOOLS

1. **MIXER** A freestanding mixer can be helpful for mixing batters and doughs. It can save a lot of time and physical effort while creating a consistent blend when working with ingredients like gelatin, starches, and coconut milk.

2. **CHEF'S KNIFE** A chef's knife is a great all-purpose knife for any at-home chef or beginner. Keeping the knife blade sharp using an at-home knife sharpener is key to getting clean cuts and having the ability to cut through thicker vegetable skins like those of squashes or rutabagas.

3. **DRY MEASURING CUPS** Dry measuring cups are best for measuring ingredients like flours, sugars, or powders. Most sets come in 1/4 cup, 1/2 cup, 3/4 cup, and 1 cup, which are standardized sizes.

4. **GLASS MEASURING CUPS** Glass measuring cups are best for measuring ingredients like water, maple syrup, and other liquid ingredients. Most glass measuring cups can measure between 1/8 cup and 2 cups, going all the way up to 8 cups.

5. **MEASURING SPOONS** Measuring spoons are great for measuring smaller quantities of both dry and liquid ingredients, such as 1 teaspoon, 1 tablespoon, and so on.

6. **CIRCLE COOKIE CUTTERS** Having circle cookie cutters on hand is a good idea when working with anti-inflammatory recipes. A lot of times these recipes are drier or wetter than traditional recipes, making it more difficult to achieve a specific look. Using cookie cutters, along with your hands and fingers, to help shape your doughs and batters can help mimic traditional recipes more closely.

7.   **WOODEN SPOON** Wooden spoons are heat resistant, making them a terrific tool to use when working with hotter sauces or other heated dishes that require stirring.

8.   **SPATULA** Spatulas are useful for scraping ingredients off the inside of a bowl or pot.

9.   **WHISK** Whisks are useful tools when not using a mixer and mixing by hand.

10.   **FINE MESH SIEVE** Fine mesh sieves are strainers that have smaller holes, allowing for more particulates to be caught in the strainer.

11.   **VEGETABLE PEELER** Vegetable peelers are useful for removing skins from vegetables and fruits.

12.   **ROLLING PIN** A rolling pin can be a helpful tool in rolling a thicker mixture, like a dough, out to a desired thickness. To prevent sticking, cassava flour can be used to dust the mixture, in combination with a rolling pin.

13.   **TONGS** Metal tongs are helpful for picking up foods while using any process that involves heat, such as frying. They come in shorter and longer lengths. When frying, it is best to use a longer set of thongs to avoid oil-splashing.

14.   **BAKING TRAY** Heavy-duty rimmed metal baking trays are best for even heat distribution during baking. They help the food cook evenly.

15. **CAST-IRON SKILLET** Cast-iron skillets are very durable. They are also additional sources of iron in your diet. They help achieve a terrific sear on meats and vegetables and facilitate even cooking throughout dishes.

16. **PARCHMENT AND WAX PAPER** Parchment and wax paper are both alternatives to aluminum foil and help prevent sticking of food to baking trays. They can also help keep moisture and heat in a food while cooking.

17. **CUTTING BOARD** Wooden cutting boards are very durable and will not leave any small shards of plastic in food. A cutting board with a thin groove around the edge helps keep any water or juices from spilling out on the counter when cutting.

18. **BLENDER** Blenders are very helpful tools when cooking for an anti-inflammatory and autoimmune diet. They help achieve smooth consistencies and break up large or hard chunks of ingredients. Getting a strong and durable blender is a great idea when cooking and baking.

19. **POTS** Metal pots can come in small and large sizes. Depending on the size of the recipe you are cooking, you may want to use a smaller or larger pot. A recipe will call for a particular size.

20. **BAKING DISH** Baking dishes are a great way to seal in moisture while baking in the oven. They can be used to help keep a dish's shape while cooking or baking as well.

SPECIAL INGREDIENTS

1. COCONUT MILK Coconut milk can come in a can or carton. When choosing a coconut milk, always ensure the coconut milk does not contain any gums like gellan gum or processed sugars. Coconut milk from a can has more coconut fat in it, so it is best used for thicker recipes like sauces. Coconut milk from a carton has less coconut fat in it, so it is best used for thinner recipes like smoothies or other thinner viscosity recipes.

2. TAPIOCA STARCH AND TAPIOCA FLOUR Tapioca starch and tapioca flour have the same functionality and can be used interchangeably. Tapioca starch and flour both describe the extracted starch from the cassava plant.

3. AIP-FRIENDLY EGG SUBSTITUTE Eggs are not anti-inflammatory or autoimmune friendly. There are autoimmune protocol (AIP)– friendly egg replacers made of tapioca starch, arrowroot powder, citrus fiber, cream of tartar, and baking soda. One brand that produces this type of egg replacer is Namaste Foods.

4. AIP-FRIENDLY CHOCOLATE CHIPS A lot of chocolate chips contain processed sugar and dairy ingredients, both of which are neither anti-inflammatory nor AIP friendly. There are multiple brands of AIP-friendly chocolate chips made of carob powder. These brands can be found online with a simple search for "carob powder chips."

5. CASSAVA FLOUR Cassava is a starchy root vegetable found in tropical regions. When dried and ground into a flour, it is a great grain-free anti-inflammatory flour substitute.

6. **TIGERNUT** Tigernuts are fibrous tubers found in the Eastern Hemisphere. Surprisingly, they are not a nut at all. They have a slight natural sweetness and can be dried whole, sliced, or ground into a flour.

7. **COCONUT FLOUR AND COCONUT FLAKES** Coconut flesh can be dried in flakes or ground into a flour. Flakes and flour will have different textures and should not be swapped out in recipes.

8. **OIL** Two great anti-inflammatory and AIP-friendly oils are avocado and coconut oil. Avocado has a very high flash point, which means that it will not burst into flames when used at high temperatures.

9. **AIP-FRIENDLY COCONUT YOGURT** Most yogurt contains processed sugars, dairy, natural flavors, and other ingredients that cause inflammation. Some coconut yogurts have coconut milk, coconut water, and probiotics as the sole ingredients; these are AIP friendly.

10. **PALM SHORTENING** Palm shortening is a great baking substitute for butter.

11. **GELATIN** Gelatin is a great gelling agent to help bind excess water in a recipe. In order to be anti-inflammatory and AIP friendly, your gelatin should be sourced from beef.

BREAKFAST

Tigernut Butter 1

Fruit Compote 3

Green Smoothie 5

Breakfast Parfait 7

Breakfast Steak Wrap 9

Breakfast Hash 11

Biscuits and Gravy 13

Waffles 15

Strawberry Banana Smoothie Bowl 16

Pancakes 18

INGREDIENTS

- 1 cup tigernuts, soaked in water as per package directions

- ¾ cup avocado oil

- ½ tsp cinnamon, ground

- 1 tsp maple syrup

- sprinkle sea salt

TIGERNUT BUTTER

SERVING SIZE 4   TIME 10 MINUTES

DIRECTIONS

1. Place all ingredients in a blender. Blend until smooth, about 8 minutes.

2. Serve at room temperature.

STORAGE

REFRIGERATOR Tigernut butter can be stored in the refrigerator for 1 month. Tigernut butter will become firm in the refrigerator and should be taken out of the refrigerator about 5 minutes prior to serving to allow the mixture to soften up and become spreadable.

INGREDIENTS

- 1 pound fruit, peeled, sliced thinly, any combination of the following will work: apples, strawberries, blackberries, raspberries, bananas, pears

- ¼ cup coconut sugar

- ½ cup apple juice, not from concentrate, no sugar added

- ½ tsp cinnamon, ground

FRUIT COMPOTE

SERVING SIZE 4   TIME 25 MINUTES

DIRECTIONS

1. Place fruit and coconut sugar in a pot.

2. Heat fruit and coconut sugar mixture on stove over low heat until fruit is soft and sugar has dissolved, about 5 minutes.

3. Add apple juice and cinnamon, turn heat up to medium, and bring mixture to a boil.

4. Once mixture is boiling, turn heat down to medium and cook mixture until fruit is either golden brown (apples, bananas, and pears) or soft (strawberries, blackberries, and raspberries), stirring occasionally with a wooden spoon so the mixture does not burn, about 10 minutes.

5. Serve warm.

STORAGE

REFRIGERATOR Fruit compote can be refrigerated for up to 1 week.

FREEZER Fruit compote can be frozen for up to 3 months.

REHEATING INSTRUCTIONS

MICROWAVE Heat on low for about 20 seconds or until warm if refrigerated or 40 seconds if frozen.

STOVE Place 1 cup of fruit compote along with 1 tbsp of water in a pot on the stove,

heat on low, stirring occasionally until warm—about 2 minutes if refrigerated or 5 minutes if frozen.

INGREDIENTS

- 2 cups coconut milk, from a carton

- ¼ cup spinach leaves

- ½ cup kale leaves, with stalks removed

- ¼ cup raspberries

- 1 banana, peeled

GREEN SMOOTHIE

SERVING SIZE 2   TIME 20 MINUTES

DIRECTIONS

1. Blend all ingredients together in a blender until smooth.

2. Portion into 2 cups.

3. Serve chilled.

STORAGE

REFRIGERATOR Green smoothies can be refrigerated for up to 1 day.

INGREDIENTS

- 2 cups AIP-friendly coconut yogurt

- 1 cup tigernuts, soaked in water as per package directions

- 1 tsp cinnamon, ground

- ½ cup water

- 2 tbsp coconut sugar

- 1 cup raspberries

BREAKFAST PARFAIT

SERVING SIZE 2   TIME 5 MINUTES

DIRECTIONS

1. Preheat oven to 350°F. Prepare a baking tray by lining it with a sheet of parchment paper.

2. Place water, cinnamon, and coconut sugar into a small pot. Bring to a boil.

3. Once water and sugar mixture is at a boil, add the tigernuts. Boil for 15 minutes or until water has evaporated.

4. Place tigernuts down on the prepared sheet tray and bake for 10 minutes in the oven or until tigernuts are lightly brown.

5. Allow tigernuts to cool completely at room temperature.

6. Place ½ cup coconut yogurt, then ¼ cup cooked tigernuts, then ¼ cup raspberries in a glass jar or other serving container. Repeat step 6 twice per serving container.

7. Serve chilled.

STORAGE

REFRIGERATOR Coconut yogurt can be stored in the refrigerator as per package instructions.

TEMPERATURE Tigernuts should be stored at room temperature in a sealed glass container for up to 1 week to keep them from becoming sticky.

INGREDIENTS

- 2 cups breakfast hash, warm; recipe on page 11

- 4 cassava flour tortilla shells at room temperature

- 1 beef tenderloin, cooked to your liking, thinly sliced, warm

BREAKFAST STEAK WRAP

SERVING SIZE 4   TIME ABOUT 10 MINUTES

DIRECTIONS

1. Spread ½ cup of breakfast hash on each tortilla shell.

2. Divide beef tenderloin into 4 portions. Lay each portion of steak on top of the breakfast hash.

3. Roll each cassava tortilla shell by folding the two sides inward while rolling the top side downward to create a wrap. Folding the two sides inward first will help keep the insides of the wrap together while eating.

4. Serve warm.

STORAGE

REFRIGERATOR Breakfast steak wrap can be refrigerated for up to 1 week.

FREEZER Breakfast steak wrap can be frozen for up to 3 months.

REHEATING INSTRUCTIONS

MICROWAVE Heat on low for about 30 seconds–1 minute or until warm if refrigerated or 1–2 minutes if frozen.

OVEN Heat oven to 350°F. Prepare a baking tray by lining it with a sheet of parchment paper. Heat breakfast steak wrap on the prepared baking tray in the oven for about 10 minutes or until warm.

INGREDIENTS

- 1¼ pounds sweet potatoes, peeled

- 6 cups water

- 1 pound bacon

- 1 yellow onion, thinly sliced

- 2 garlic cloves, small diced

- 1 tbsp onion powder

- 2 tsp garlic powder

BREAKFAST HASH

SERVING SIZE 4   TIME 40 MINUTES

DIRECTIONS

1. Place the 6 cups of water in a pot over high heat. Bring to a boil.

2. Add the sweet potatoes to the boiling water; cook until a knife can be inserted into a sweet potato and removed without the sweet potato sticking to the knife, about 25 minutes.

3. When sweet potatoes are finished cooking, remove sweet potatoes from the water, and allow to cool at room temperature.

4. While sweet potatoes are cooking and cooling, cook the bacon in a cast-iron pan over medium heat until crispy. Flip bacon over to ensure both sides of the bacon are crispy, cooking for about 4 minutes per side.

5. Once the bacon is cooked fully, remove the bacon from the cast-iron pan. Do not discard bacon grease.

6. Add the onions to the cast-iron pan that contains the bacon grease and cook over medium heat until onions are translucent, about 5 minutes. Add the garlic, onion powder, and garlic powder. Cook until garlic is crispy brown, about 3 minutes. Remove cast-iron pan from the heat.

7. Cut sweet potatoes into small bite-size pieces, about 1-inch-thick squares.

8. Cut bacon into bite-size pieces.

9. Add the cut sweet potatoes and bacon to the onion and garlic mixture in the cast-iron pan.

10. Serve warm.

STORAGE

REFRIGERATOR Breakfast hash can be refrigerated for up to 1 week.

FREEZER Breakfast hash can be frozen for up to 3 months.

REHEATING INSTRUCTIONS

MICROWAVE Heat on low for about 1–2 minutes or until warm if refrigerated or 3–4 minutes if frozen.

STOVE Place 1 cup of breakfast hash, ½ tsp of avocado or coconut oil, and 1 tbsp of water in a cast-iron pan on the stove, heat on low, stirring occasionally until warm, about 2 minutes if refrigerated or 5 minutes if frozen.

INGREDIENTS

- 1 recipe biscuits; recipe on page 156

- 1 pound organic grass-fed ground beef

- 1 yellow onion, small diced

- 1 tbsp avocado oil

- 1 tsp sea salt

- 2 cups mother sauce, recipe on page 136

BISCUITS AND GRAVY

SERVING SIZE 4   TIME 30 MINUTES

DIRECTIONS

1. Heat a cast-iron skillet over medium heat until warm, about 2 minutes.

2. Add onions and avocado oil to the cast iron pan. Cook over medium heat until onions are golden brown, about 5 minutes, stirring occasionally with a wooden spoon.

3. Add ground beef and salt to the onions. Cook until ground beef is fully cooked through, stirring occasionally, about 10 minutes. Ground beef will change from a pink color to a grayish-brown color when fully cooked through.

4. Add the mother sauce to the beef and onion mixture. Heat over medium heat until mixture is fully warm, stirring occasionally with a wooden spoon, about 10 minutes.

5. Cook biscuits according to biscuit recipe directions.

6. Pour gravy over warm biscuits.

7. Serve warm; enjoy!

STORAGE

REFRIGERATOR Gravy can be refrigerated for up to 1 week. Biscuits, once fully cooked, should be frozen. Fully cooked biscuits will become soggy if stored in the refrigerator.

FREEZER Biscuits and gravy can be frozen for up to 3 months. Biscuits and gravy should be stored separately in the freezer to avoid biscuits becoming soggy in the gravy.

REHEATING INSTRUCTIONS

MICROWAVE For refrigerated gravy, heat on low for about 1–2 minutes or until warm. For frozen biscuits and gravy, microwave together for about 1–2 minutes or until warm.

STOVE Place 1 cup of gravy, along with 1 tbsp of water, in a cast-iron pan on the stove; heat on low, stirring occasionally until warm, about 2 minutes if refrigerated or 5 minutes if frozen. Biscuits can be reheated in the oven at 350°F for about 10 minutes or until warm.

INGREDIENTS

- 1 plantain, skin removed
- ⅔ cup tigernuts, soaked as per package directions
- ½ cup arrowroot flour
- ½ cup tigernut flour
- ½ cup cassava flour
- ¼ cup coconut flour
- 3 tbsp maple syrup
- ½ tsp sea salt
- 1 tsp cream of tartar
- 1½ tsp baking soda
- 2 tsp baking powder
- 1 tsp cinnamon, ground
- 2 tsp vanilla extract
- 3 cup water
- 1 tsp coconut oil

WAFFLES

SERVING SIZE 4   TIME 45 MINUTES

DIRECTIONS

1. Heat a waffle iron as per machine instructions until warm.

2. While the waffle iron is heating up, place all the ingredients in a blender to make the waffle batter. Blend until smooth, about 4 minutes.

3. Once it is heated, lightly spray the waffle iron with coconut oil spray to avoid waffle batter from sticking.

4. Portion ¼ cup–½ cup of waffle batter onto the waffle iron, depending on the size of the waffle iron. Cook until done. Timing of doneness will depend on given waffle iron. Follow machine instructions for timing.

5. Serve warm.

STORAGE

REFRIGERATOR Waffles can be refrigerated for up to 2 days.

FREEZER Waffles can be frozen for up to 3 months.

REHEATING INSTRUCTIONS

MICROWAVE Heat on low for about 10–20 seconds or until warm if refrigerated or 30 seconds–1 minute if frozen.

OVEN Heat oven to 350°F. Prepare a baking tray by lining it with a sheet of parchment paper. Heat waffles in the oven on the prepared baking tray for 10 minutes or until warm.

STRAWBERRY BANANA SMOOTHIE BOWL

SERVING SIZE 2   TIME 10 MINUTES

INGREDIENTS

- 2 cups coconut milk, from a carton

- 1 cups ice

- 6 strawberries, tops trimmed off

- 2 bananas, peeled

- 1 cup AIP-friendly coconut yogurt

OPTIONAL TOPPINGS

- sliced strawberries

- sliced bananas

- coconut flakes, unsweetened

DIRECTIONS

1.   Place all ingredients in a blender and blend until smooth, about 5 minutes.

2.   Portion into 2 bowls and top with optional toppings.

3.   Serve immediately to maintain frozen texture.

STORAGE

REFRIGERATOR Strawberry banana smoothie bowls can be refrigerated for up to 1 day.

PANCAKES

SERVING SIZE 4   TIME 40 MINUTES

INGREDIENTS

- 1 ½ cups tigernut flour

- 6 tbsp tapioca starch/flour

- ½ cup coconut flour

- pinch sea salt

- 1 ½ tsp baking soda

- 2 ¾ cups coconut milk, from a can

- ½ tsp baking powder

- 3 tsp white balsamic vinegar

- 3 ½ tbsp maple syrup

- 6 tbsp cassava flour

- 1 tsp vanilla extract

- ½ tsp cinnamon, ground

- ¼ tsp nutmeg, ground

- 2 tsp AIP egg substitute + 4 tbsp water

- coconut oil spray

DIRECTIONS

1.   Combine tigernut flour, tapioca starch/flour, coconut flour, salt, baking soda, baking powder, cassava flour, cinnamon, and nutmeg in the bowl of a mixer. Mix on low speed using a whisk attachment until fully dispersed, about 2 minutes.

2.   In a separate bowl, combine the egg substitute with the 16 g of water. Whisk until combined, about 20 seconds.

3.   Add the egg replacement mixture, maple syrup, vanilla, vinegar, and coconut milk to the mixing bowl. Mix on low speed using the whisk attachment until smooth, about 4 minutes.

4.   While the mixture is mixing, heat a cast iron pan over medium heat until warm.

5.   Lightly spray the cast-iron pan using coconut oil spray. Spoon ¼ cup pancake batter onto the sprayed and heated cast-iron pan. Lightly pray the back of a spoon with coconut oil spray and spread the pancake batter out into a circle that is about 2 cm high. Cook over medium low heat until the top of the pancake is bubbling slightly.

6.   Carefully flip pancake over using a metal spatula. Cook pancake over medium low heat until the center is fully cooked through, about 3 minutes. Center will still be semimoist but not completely wet and batterlike.

7.   Serve warm.

REHEATING INSTRUCTIONS

REFRIGERATOR Preheat oven to 350°F. Prepare a baking tray by lining it with 1 sheet of parchment paper. Place pancakes on the prepared baking tray. Cook in the oven until warm, about 5 minutes.

FREEZER Preheat oven to 350°F. Prepare a baking tray by lining it with 1 sheet of parchment paper. Place pancakes on the prepared baking tray. Cook in the oven until warm, about 5 minutes.

STORAGE

REFRIGERATOR Pancakes can be refrigerated for up to 1 week.

FREEZER Pancakes can be frozen for up to 4 months.

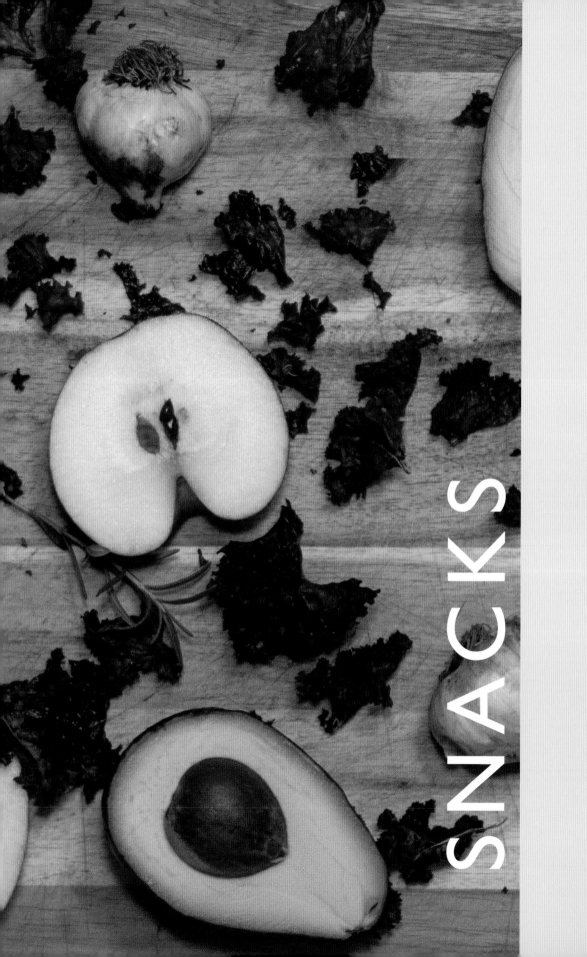

SNACKS

Ants on a Log............................ 22

Apple Granola Slices..................... 23

Frozen Blueberry Bites................... 25

Guacamole 27

Kale Chips 29

Pineapple Strawberry Salsa............... 31

Rutabaga Beet Dip........................ 32

Tortilla Chips........................... 35

ANTS ON A LOG

SERVING SIZE 4   TIME 10 MINUTES

INGREDIENTS

- 4 celery stalks, cut in half

- 8 tbsp tigernut butter; recipe on page 1

- 2 tbsp dried cranberries or raisins, no sugar added

DIRECTIONS

1.   Using a butter knife, spread tigernut butter across center of celery sticks.

2.   Top tigernut butter with dried cranberries or raisins.

3.   Serve at room temperature.

STORAGE

REFRIGERATOR Ants on a log can be stored in the refrigerator for up to 2 days.

APPLE GRANOLA SLICES

SERVING SIZE 2   TIME 30 MINUTES

INGREDIENTS

- ½ cup water

- ½ tsp cinnamon, ground

- ¼ cup coconut sugar

- sprinkle sea salt

- 1 apple, any variety, with skin on, sliced into about 1/2-inch slices

- 2 tbsp tigernut butter, recipe on page 1

- 1 cup tigernuts, rehydrated as per package directions

DIRECTIONS

1. Heat oven to 325°F. Prepare a baking tray by lining it with 1 sheet of parchment paper.

2. Place water, cinnamon, sugar, and salt in a medium-sized pot on the stove over high heat. Bring ingredients to a boil, then add the tigernuts, about 5 minutes.

3. Continue to boil the ingredients until all the water has evaporated, about 8 minutes.

4. Place tigernuts on the prepared baking tray and bake in the oven for 5 minutes or until golden brown.

5. Remove the baking tray from the oven and allow to cool completely.

6. Spread the tigernut butter across the tops of the apple slices. Top the tigernut butter with the baked tigernut pieces.

7. Serve at room temperature.

STORAGE

REFRIGERATOR Apple granola slices can be stored in the refrigerator for up to 2 days.

INGREDIENTS

- 1 pint blueberries

- 2 cups AIP-friendly coconut yogurt

- 6 wooden skewers

FROZEN BLUEBERRY BITES

SERVING SIZE 6   TIME 30 MINUTES

DIRECTIONS

1.   Prepare a baking tray by lining it with 1 sheet of parchment paper.

2.   Skewer 8 blueberries on each wooden skewer.

3.   Using a pastry brush, brush coconut yogurt over each blueberry, coating them from front to back.

4.   Place each skewer on the prepared baking tray.

5.   Place baking tray in the freezer for at least 25 minutes or until fully frozen through.

6.   Serve frozen.

VARIATIONS

This recipe can be made with other fruits as well, like strawberries, raspberries, or blackberries.

STORAGE

FREEZER Frozen blueberry bites can be stored in the freezer for up to 2 months.

INGREDIENTS

- 5 avocados, skin and seed removed, flesh scooped out

- 2 tbsp white balsamic vinegar

- ¼ red onion, rough chopped

- ¼ cup avocado oil

- 2 tsp sea salt

- 2 tsp onion powder

- 1 tsp garlic powder

- 1 garlic clove

- ¼ cup parsley, fresh

GUACAMOLE

SERVING SIZE 6   TIME 10 MINUTES

DIRECTIONS

1.   Place all ingredients in a blender and blend until smooth, about 5 minutes.

2.   Serve at room temperature or cold.

STORAGE

REFRIGERATOR Guacamole can be stored in the refrigerator for up to 1 week. The top of the guacamole will naturally turn brown; this does not mean the guacamole is bad. The top can be scooped off and the remaining guacamole can be served.

INGREDIENTS

- 1 bunch kale, stems removed, leaves roughly chopped into about 1-inch-thick pieces

- coconut oil spray

- 1 tsp sea salt

KALE CHIPS

SERVING SIZE 4   TIME 15 MINUTES

DIRECTIONS

1. Heat oven to 325°F. Prepare a baking tray by lining it with 1 sheet of parchment paper.

2. Place the kale leaf pieces on the prepared baking tray.

3. Spray enough coconut oil on top of the kale leaves to thoroughly coat them.

4. Sprinkle with the sea salt.

5. Toss the kale leaves together to evenly coat each piece.

6. Place the baking tray in the oven. Cook for 10 minutes.

7. Using a spatula, toss the kale leaves around on the sheet tray to ensure the pieces are cooking evenly. Spray the kale leaves lightly with coconut oil.

8. Continue cooking until the kale is dried and crispy, about 3 minutes. Kale chips cook quickly, so be sure to monitor the chips closely to prevent burning in the oven.

STORAGE

ROOM TEMPERATURE Kale chips can be kept at room temperature in an airtight container for up to 2 weeks.

INGREDIENTS

- ½ pineapple, skin removed, diced into small bite-sized pieces

- ½ yellow onion, diced

- 1 pint strawberries, tops removed, chopped

- ⅛ tsp sea salt

- ½ tsp coconut sugar

- ¼ tsp onion powder

- 1/2 tsp white balsamic vinegar

PINEAPPLE STRAWBERRY SALSA

SERVING SIZE 4   TIME 20 MINUTES

DIRECTIONS

1. Toss all ingredients together in a medium-sized bowl.

2. Cover the bowl and place it in the refrigerator for 1 hour to marinate.

3. Serve cold or at room temperature.

STORAGE

REFRIGERATOR Pineapple strawberry salsa can be stored in the refrigerator for up to 1 week.

RUTABAGA BEET DIP

SERVING SIZE 4   TIME I HOUR 20 MINUTES

INGREDIENTS

- 2 pounds rutabaga, peeled, chopped into 1-inch-thick pieces

- 1 pound beets, peeled, chopped into 1-inch-thick pieces

- ½ cup avocado oil

- 1 tsp sea salt

- 1 tsp white balsamic vinegar

- 6 cups water

- 2 tbsp sea salt

DIRECTIONS

I.   Place 6 cups of water and 2 tbsp of salt in a large pot over high heat on the stove. Bring to a boil, about 10 minutes.

2.   Add the rutabaga to the boiling water. Cook until fork-tender, about 30 minutes.

3.   Remove rutabaga from the water; do not discard water or turn off heat.

4.   Add the beets to the boiling water. Cook until fork-tender, about 20 minutes.

5.   Remove beets from the water. Discard the water.

6. Add the rutabaga, beets, avocado oil, 1 tsp salt, and white balsamic vinegar to a blender. Blend until smooth, about 5 minutes.

7. Allow mixture to cool completely. Serve chilled.

STORAGE

REFRIGERATOR Rutabaga beet dip can be stored in the refrigerator for up to 2 weeks.

TORTILLA CHIPS

SERVING SIZE 6   TIME 40 MINUTES

DIRECTIONS

1. Place the avocado oil in a large cast-iron pan on the stove over medium-high heat. Heat the oil until it reaches 365°F.

2. Place the cassava shell triangles into the oil. Do not overcrowd the pan; this may take a couple rounds of cooking.

3. Cook the cassava shell triangles in the oil until first side is slightly golden brown, about 30 seconds.

4. Using tongs, flip the tortilla triangles over and cook for 20 seconds.

5. Remove cassava shell triangles from the oil and place on a paper towel–lined plate. Sprinkle the tops of the casava shell triangles with sea salt while still hot.

6. Repeat steps 2–5 until all triangles are cooked.

7. Serve warm or at room temperature.

STORAGE

ROOM TERMPERATURE Tortilla chips are best eaten within a couple hours of cooking but can be kept at room temperature for up to 1 week.

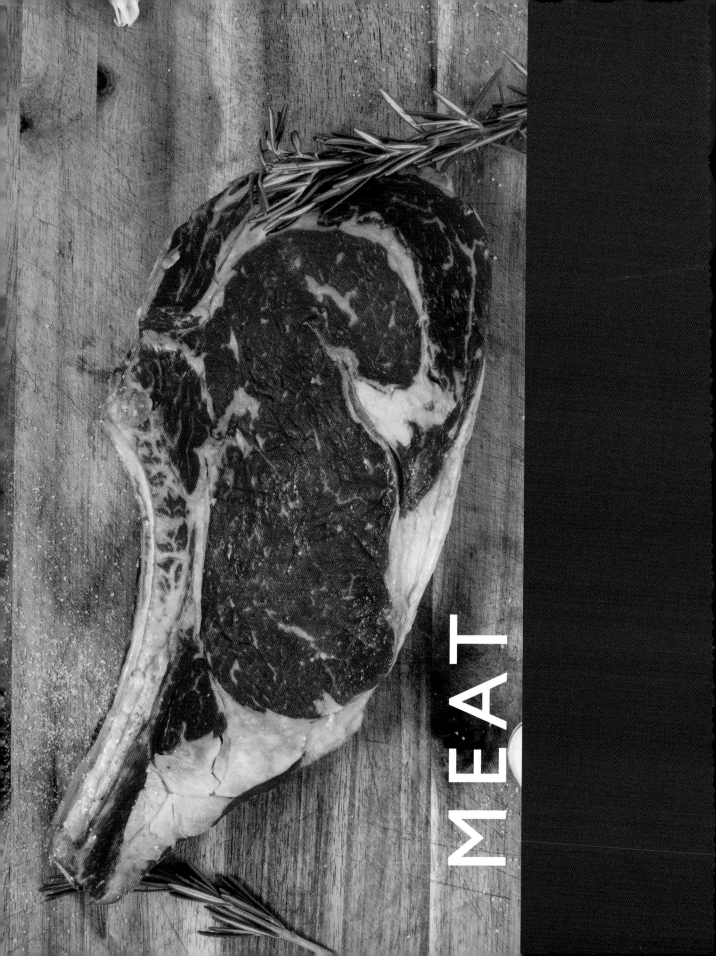

MEAT

Burgers. 39

Chicken Pesto Pasta Salad 40

Chicken Pot Pie 42

Chicken Tenders 45

Crackling Pork Roast with Blackberry Sauce . . . 46

Korean BBQ Steak 49

Thanksgiving Turkey 50

Meatballs 53

Pork Tenderloin. 55

Sautéed Chicken Breast 57

Sautéed Pork Chops 59

INGREDIENTS

- 1 lb. ground beef, grass-fed

- 1 red onion, small diced

- 1 garlic clove, small diced

- 2 tsp onion powder

- 1 tsp garlic powder

- ¼ cup parsley, chopped

- 2 tsp sea salt

BURGERS

SERVING SIZE 6   TIME 45 MINUTES

DIRECTIONS

1. Combine all ingredients in a large bowl. Using a wooden spoon, mix ingredients together until fully combined, about 2 minutes.

2. Portion mixture into 6 balls. Using your hands, flatten each ball into 1½-inch-thick discs.

3. Cook burgers either in the oven, on the grill, or on the stove.

4. To cook burgers in the oven: Preheat oven to 400°F. Prepare a baking tray by lining it with a sheet of parchment paper. Place burger patties on the prepared baking tray. Place baking tray in the oven and cook for about 15 minutes or until burger insides register at 160°F for well done, 150°F for medium well, 140°F for medium, and 130°F for medium rare.

5. To cook burgers on the grill: Heat grill to 300°F, place burgers on indirectly, flipping burgers over every 30 minutes. Cook burgers until the inside registers at 160°F for well done, 150°F for medium well, 140°F for medium, and 130°F for medium rare.

6. To cook burgers on the stove: Heat a cast-iron pan on the stove over medium heat until warm. Place burgers on the warm cast-iron pan, flipping every 3 minutes. Cook burgers until the inside registers at 160°F for well done, 150°F for medium well, 140°F for medium, and 130°F for medium rare.

STORAGE

REFRIGERATOR Burgers can be kept in the refrigerator for up to 4 days after cooking.

FREEZER Burgers can be kept in the freezer for up to 1 month after cooking.

REHEATING INSTRUCTIONS

REFRIGERATOR Place burgers in a cast iron pan with 1 tbsp water. Place cast-iron pan on the stove over medium-low heat and cook until warm, about 3 minutes.

FREEZER Place burgers in a cast-iron pan with 1 tbsp water. Place cast-iron pan on the stove over medium-low heat and cook until warm, about 10 minutes.

CHICKEN PESTO PASTA SALAD

SERVING SIZE 4   TIME 10 MINUTES

INGREDIENTS

- 4 tbsp pesto; recipe on page 141

- 1 recipe pasta; recipe on page 162

- 1 recipe chicken breast, chicken cut into bite sized pieces

- 1 tbsp white balsamic vinegar

DIRECTIONS

1.   Place pesto and chicken together in a large bowl. Using a wooden spoon, toss pesto and chicken together until chicken is fully coated in pesto, about 2 minutes.

2.   Add pasta and vinegar to the chicken pesto mixture. Using a wooden spoon, gently toss mixture until evenly dispersed, about 2 minutes.

3.   Serve at room temperature.

STORAGE

REFRIGERATOR Chicken pesto pasta salad can be stored in the refrigerator for up to 1 week.

FREEZER Chicken pesto pasta salad can be stored in the freezer for up to 1 month.

REHEATING INSTRUCTIONS

REFRIGERATOR Place 1 cup chicken pesto pasta salad in a pot with 1 tbsp of water. Place the pot on the stove over medium-low heat and cook until warm, about 2 minutes.

FREEZER Place 1 cup chicken pesto pasta salad in a pot with 1 tbsp of water. Place the pot on the stove over medium-low heat and cook until warm, about 10 minutes.

CHICKEN POT PIE

SERVING SIZE 6   TIME 45 MINUTES

INGREDIENTS

- 1 recipe biscuits; recipe on page 156

- 1 recipe chicken (recipe on page 57), cut into bite-size pieces

- 1/2 pound parsnips, peeled, cut into bite-size pieces

- 1/2 pound carrots, peeled, cut into bite-size pieces

- 3 celery stalks, sliced thin

- 5 cups chicken stock

- 2 cups mother sauce (recipe on page 136), at room temperature

- 2 tbsp avocado oil

DIRECTIONS

1. Heat oven to 325°F.

2. Pour the chicken stock and mother sauce into a 8 x 11 inch glass baking dish. Using a whisk, whisk the chicken stock and mother sauce together until fully combined, about 1 minute.

3. Add parsnips, carrots, celery, and chicken into the baking dish. Using a wooden spoon, stir ingredients into the stock and mother sauce mixture until vegetables and chicken pieces are evenly coated, about 2 minutes.

4. Portion biscuit dough into about 10 small dough balls. Gently flatten biscuit dough balls by hand until about 1/4 inch thick.

5. Place biscuit rounds on top of chicken and vegetable mixture. Brush tops of biscuits with avocado oil.

6. Place baking dish in the oven. Bake until vegetables are fork-tender and biscuit dough is golden brown on top, about 15 minutes.

7. Serve warm.

STORAGE

REFRIGERATOR Chicken pot pie can be stored in the refrigerator for up to 1 week.

FREEZER Chicken pot pie can be stored in the freezer for up to 2 months.

REHEATING INSTRUCTIONS

REFRIGERATOR Preheat the oven to 350°F. Place the chicken pot pie in a glass baking dish. Place the baking dish in the oven and cook until chicken pot pie is warm, about 10–15 minutes.

FREEZER Preheat the oven to 350°F. Place the chicken pot pie in a glass baking dish. Place the baking dish in the oven and cook until chicken pot pie is warm, about 25–30 minutes.

INGREDIENTS

- 2 pounds chicken tenders
- 6 cups avocado oil

COCONUT MILK MIXTURE:

- 3 cups coconut milk
- 1 tsp garlic powder
- 2 tsp onion powder

- 1 tsp dill weed, dried
- 2 tsp sea salt

CASSAVA FLOUR MIXTURE:

- 4 cups cassava flour
- 1 tsp sea salt

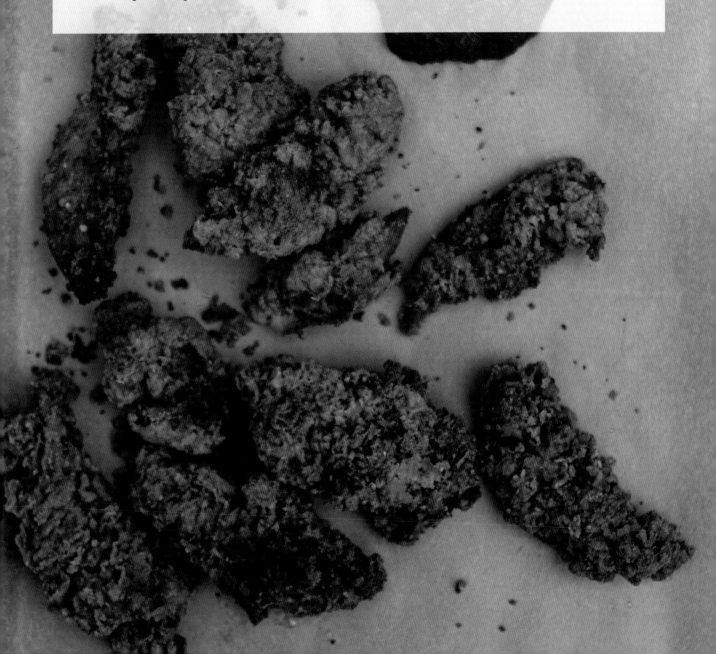

CHICKEN TENDERS

SERVING SIZE 5   TIME I HOUR

DIRECTIONS

1. Place avocado oil in a large cast-iron pan. Heat pan over medium heat on the stove until a thermometer inserted into the oil reads 375°F.

2. While the oil is heating, make the coconut milk mixture by placing all the coconut milk mixture ingredients into a large bowl. Using a whisk, whisk the ingredients together until there are no clumps and mixture is smooth, about 2 minutes.

3. While the oil is heating, make the cassava flour mixture by placing all ingredients in a medium bowl, and whisk until fully combined, about 30 seconds.

4. Once oil is at temperature, dip the tenders in the coconut milk mixture and then in the cassava flour mixture. Repeat this step so that tenders are dipped in the coconut milk mixture and the cassava flour mixture twice.

5. Place tenders in the hot oil carefully. Only place about 4–5 tenders in the pan at a time; the number will depend on pan size. Do not overcrowd the pan or the tenders will not cook properly.

6. Allow tenders to cook until golden brown on the bottom; flip and allow to cook until golden brown on the opposite side, about 5–8 minutes per side. While cooking the tenders, keep checking on the oil temperature to ensure it remains at 375°F. Turn heat up or down as needed to maintain temperature.

7. Once chicken tenders are done cooking, remove the tenders from the oil and place on a paper towel to remove excess oil.

8. Serve warm.

STORAGE

FREEZER Tenders can be cooled completely and stored in an airtight container in the freezer for up to 3 months. The freezer is best for storing chicken tenders as they will become soggy in the refrigerator.

REHEATING INSTRUCTIONS

FREEZER Heat oven to 350°F. Prepare a baking tray by lining it with 1 sheet of parchment paper. Place chicken tenders on the prepared baking tray. Place baking tray in the oven and cook just until chicken tenders are warm, about 15 minutes.

CRACKLING PORK ROAST WITH BLACKBERRY SAUCE

SERVING SIZE 5   TIME 17—22 HOURS

INGREDIENTS

- 4 cups brine; recipe on page 118

- 4 pounds pork rib roast

- ½ cup coconut sugar

- 2 tbsp honey

- 2 cups blackberry sauce, warm; recipe on page 117

DIRECTIONS

1. Place pork rib roast in a large pot with the brine. Cover pot with a lid. Let pork rib roast side in the brine for 12 hours—16 at most—in the refrigerator. This will allow the meat to become tender from the brine.

2. After resting pork rib roast in the refrigerator, discard the brine and place the pork rib roast back in the pot. Cover the pot and place the pot back in the refrigerator for an additional 4 hours without the brine.

3. Heat the oven to 250°F.

4. After resting the pork rib roast for the additional 4 hours in the refrigerator, rub the skin of the pork rib roast with the coconut sugar and honey.

5. Place pork rib roast in a medium-sized roasting pan and cook covered in the oven until the internal temperature of the pork reaches 135°F, about 2 hours.

6. Remove the pork rib roast from the oven and let rest, uncovered, for 30 minutes.

7. While the pork rib roast is resting, increase oven temperature to 450°F.

8. Place the pork rib roast back in the oven and cook uncovered until the skin is crispy brown, about 10–20 minutes.

9. Remove the pork rib roast from the oven and let rest, uncovered, for 5 minutes.

10. To serve, carve roast between bones and pour blackberry sauce over top.

STORAGE

REFRIGERATOR Crackling pork roast with blackberry sauce can be kept in the refrigerator for up to 1 week.

FREEZER Crackling pork roast with blackberry sauce can be kept in the freezer for up to 2 months.

REHEATING INSTRUCTIONS

REFRIGERATOR Place crackling pork roast with blackberry sauce in a pot with a drizzle of water. Place pot on the stove over medium heat. Heat until warm, about 5 minutes.

FREEZER Place crackling pork roast with blackberry sauce in a pot with a drizzle of water. Place pot on the stove over medium heat. Heat until warm, about 13 minutes.

INGREDIENTS

- 2 pounds flank steak

- 3 cups Korean barbecue sauce; recipe on page 135

- 4 pears, skin removed, core removed, pureed in a blender

- 4 tbsp coconut oil

KOREAN BBQ STEAK

SERVING SIZE 4   TIME 26 HOURS

DIRECTIONS

1. Place pureed pears and flank steak in a large glass baking dish. Rub the pear puree on all sides of the steak. Cover the top of the baking dish with plastic wrap and refrigerate for 24 hours.

2. Once steak has marinated in the pear puree for 24 hours, remove pear puree from the flank steak by scraping it off with a knife. Discard puree.

3. Pour 1 cup of Korean barbecue sauce over the flank steak. Using your hands, rub the Korean barbecue sauce into the flank steak.

4. Heat a large cast-iron pan on the stove over medium high heat until warm, about 4 minutes.

5. Add the coconut oil to the heated cast-iron pan, followed by the flank steak. Cook one side of the flank steak until golden brown, about 5 minutes. Using tongs, flip the flank steak to cook the opposite side and cook until golden brown, about 5 minutes. Continue to cook flank steak, flipping occasionally, until internal temperature reads 145°F.

6. Once internal temperature of the flank steak reaches 145°F, brush 1 cup of Korean barbecue sauce over all sides of the meat.

7. Remove flank steak from cast-iron pan, and allow to cool for 5 minutes at room temperature.

8. To serve, slice Korean barbecue steak thinly. Serve warm. Serve the remaining Korean barbecue sauce on the side for dipping.

STORAGE

REFRIGERATOR Korean barbecue steak can be kept in the refrigerator for up to 4 days.

FREEZER Korean barbecue steak can be kept in the refrigerator for up to 1 month.

REHEATING INSTRUCTIONS

REFRIGERATOR Place Korean barbecue steak with a drizzle of water in a pot. Place the pot on the stove and heat over medium-low heat until warm, about 3 minutes.

FREEZER Place Korean barbecue steak with a drizzle of water in a pot. Place the pot on the stove and heat over medium-low heat until warm, about 6 minutes.

THANKSGIVING TURKEY

SERVING SIZE 8   TIME 4 HOURS

INGREDIENTS

- 1 recipe turkey brine, cooled; recipe on page 118
- 20 pound whole bird turkey, thawed
- ¼ cup avocado oil
- 1 tsp Herbs de Provence seasoning
- 4 celery stalks, sliced thin

- 1 onion, chopped
- 2 garlic cloves, chopped
- 2 carrots, peeled, sliced thin
- 1 pomegranate, quartered
- 2 cups chicken stock

DIRECTIONS

1. Place the turkey brine in a large pot with the turkey. Place the pot in the refrigerator for 12–14 hours.

2. Preheat oven to 350°F. Remove turkey from the brine. Discard the brine.

3. Rinse the turkey under cold running water for 1 minute.

4. Place the celery, onion, garlic, carrots, pomegranate, and chicken stock in the bottom of a roasting pan.

5. Place the turkey on top of the vegetable mix in the roasting pan. Rub the turkey with avocado oil and Herbs de Provence seasoning.

6. Cover the turkey with a sheet of parchment paper. Place the roasting pan with the turkey in the oven.

7. Cook the turkey for a total of 4 hours or until the center of the turkey reads 165°F with a thermometer inserted into the thickest part of the turkey meat.

8. While turkey is cooking, using a baster, baste the turkey every 30 minutes by removing the parchment paper and pouring some of the liquid in the bottom of the roasting pan over the top of the

turkey. Before continuing to cook the turkey, place the sheet of parchment paper back over the turkey.

9.   Once the turkey reaches 165°F, remove the sheet of parchment paper from the top of the turkey and turn the oven to high broil.

10.   Cook the turkey in the oven on the broil setting until the top turns golden brown, about 1–2 minutes. Ensure a close eye is kept on the turkey during this step as broil settings on an oven can cook food very quickly.

11.   Once the turkey top is golden brown, remove the turkey from the oven and allow it to rest at room temperature for 20 minutes prior to carving.

12.   Serve warm.

STORAGE

REFRIGERATOR Turkey can be stored in the refrigerator for up to 1 week.

REHEATING INSTRUCTIONS

REFRIGERATOR Place the turkey in a pot with a drizzle of water on the stove over low heat. Cook turkey over low heat until warm, about 3 minutes.

INGREDIENTS

- 1 yellow onion, diced

- 1 pound ground beef, grass-fed

- 4 garlic cloves, minced

- 1 tsp sea salt

- 4 tbsp bacon fat

- 2 tsp onion powder

- 1 tsp garlic powder

MEATBALLS

SERVING SIZE 6   TIME 2 HOURS

DIRECTIONS

1. Heat oven to 350°F. Prepare a baking tray by lining it with 1 sheet of parchment paper.

2. In a large bowl, mix all the ingredients together with a wooden spoon or by hand until all ingredients are evenly dispersed, about 4 minutes.

3. Using your hands, form the meat mixture into 3 tbsp portions. Using your hands, roll each portion into small balls to form meatballs.

4. Place the meatballs onto the prepared baking tray. Place baking tray in the oven.

5. Bake meatballs in the oven for 30 minutes or until center of meatballs are fully brown in color without any pink color to them. Remove the baking tray from the oven.

6. Turn on the oven broiler.

7. Once broiler is ready, place baking tray back in the oven. Broil until the tops of the meatballs are golden brown, about 2–3 minutes. Remove baking tray from the oven.

8. Serve warm.

STORAGE

REFRIGERATOR Meatballs can be stored in the refrigerator for up to 1 week.

FREEZER Meatballs can be stored in the freezer for up to 3 months.

REHEATING INSTRUCTIONS

REFRIGERATOR Heat oven to 350°F. Prepare a baking tray by lining it with 1 sheet of parchment paper. Place meatballs on the prepared baking tray. Place baking tray in the oven and cook meatballs until warm, about 5–10 minutes.

FREEZER Heat oven to 350°F. Prepare a baking tray by lining it with 1 sheet of parchment paper. Place meatballs on the prepared baking tray. Place baking tray in the oven and cook meatballs until warm, about 15–20 minutes.

INGREDIENTS

- 1 pound pork tenderloin

- 1 tsp sea salt

- 2 tsp onion powder

- 1 tsp garlic powder

- 1 tsp coconut sugar

PORK TENDERLOIN

SERVING SIZE 4   TIME 30 MINUTES

DIRECTIONS

1. Sprinkle spices and coconut sugar over all sides of the pork tenderloin.

2. Cook pork tenderloin on the grill or sauté on the stove top.

    GRILL Heat grill to 350°F with indirect heat. Grill pork tenderloin over indirect heat until the internal temperature reads 140°F, about 30 minutes. Remove pork tenderloin from the grill and allow to cool at room temperature for 20 minutes. When pork is taken off of heat at 140°F, it will carry over to a 145°F internal temperature. Slice into 1-inch-thick slices; serve warm.

    SAUTÉ Heat a large cast-iron pan on the stove over medium heat until warm, about 5 minutes. Add avocado oil to warm cast-iron pan, followed by pork tenderloin. Cook until bottom side of pork tenderloin is golden brown, about 5 minutes. Using tongs, flip pork tenderloin over and cook opposite side until it is golden brown and internal temperature reads 140°F, about 10 minutes. Remove pork tenderloin from the cast-iron pan and allow to cool at room temperature for 20 minutes. When pork is taken off of heat at 140°F, it will carry over to a 145°F internal temperature. Slice into 1-inch-thick slices; serve warm.

STORAGE

REFRIGERATOR Pork tenderloin can be stored in the refrigerator for up to 4 days.

FREEZER Pork tenderloin can be stored in the freezer for up to 1 month.

REHEATING INSTRUCTIONS

REFRIGERATOR Heat oven to 350°F. Prepare a baking tray by lining it with 1 sheet of parchment paper. Place the pork tenderloin on the prepared baking tray. Place the baking tray in the oven and heat until pork tenderloin is warm, about 10 minutes.

FREEZER Heat oven to 350°F. Prepare a baking tray by lining it with 1 sheet of parchment paper. Place the pork tenderloin on the prepared baking tray. Place the baking tray in the oven and heat until pork tenderloin is warm, about 15–20 minutes.

INGREDIENTS

- 4 chicken breasts, bone in, with skin still on

- 2 tbsp sea salt

- 1 tsp garlic powder

- 1 tsp onion powder

- 4 tbsp avocado oil

SAUTÉED CHICKEN BREAST

SERVING SIZE 4   TIME 40 MINUTES

DIRECTIONS

1. Heat large cast-iron pan on the stove over medium heat until warm, about 6 minutes.

2. While the cast-iron pan is warming, sprinkle spices and sea salt over the chicken breast skin. Using your hands, rub the spices and salt into the chicken breast skin.

3. Drizzle the avocado oil into the heated cast-iron pan.

4. Place chicken skin side down into the cast-iron pan and cook until the skin is crispy and golden brown, about 5 minutes.

5. Using tongs, flip chicken over and cook opposite side of chicken until the internal temperature reads 165°F. Remove the chicken from the cast-iron pan.

6. Serve warm.

STORAGE

REFRIGERATOR Sautéed chicken can be kept in the refrigerator for up to 1 week.

FREEZER Sautéed chicken can be kept in the freezer for up to 1 week.

REHEATING INSTRUCTIONS

REFRIGERATOR Place sautéed chicken with a drizzle of water in a pot. Place pot on the stove over medium-low heat and cook until sautéed chicken is warm, about 5 minutes.

FREEZER Place sautéed chicken with a drizzle of water in a pot. Place pot on the stove over medium-low heat and cook until sautéed chicken is warm, about 10 minutes.

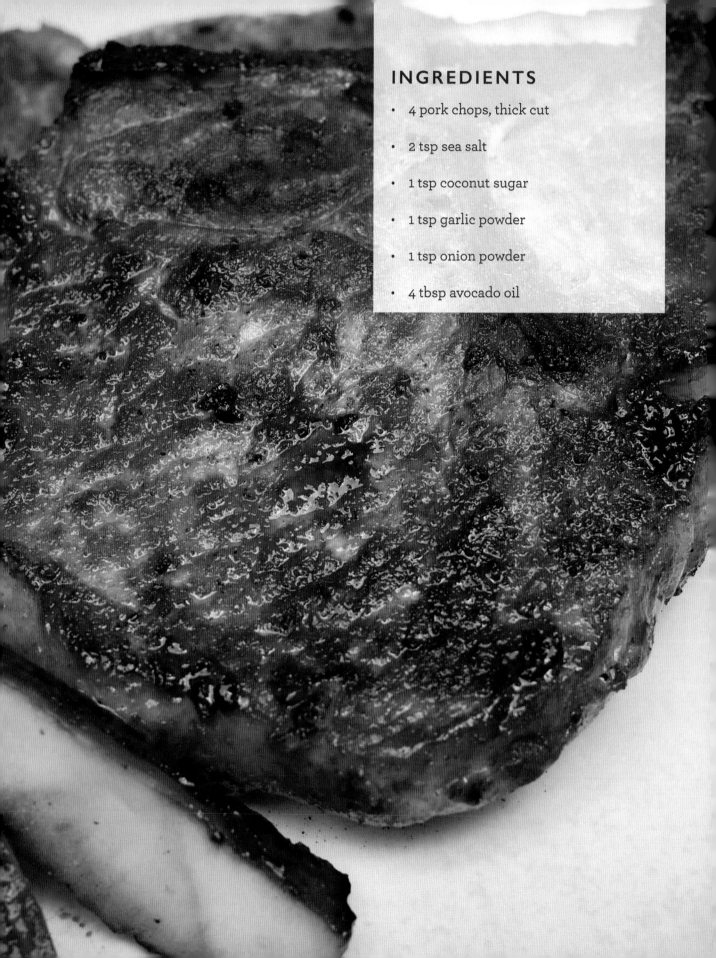

INGREDIENTS

- 4 pork chops, thick cut

- 2 tsp sea salt

- 1 tsp coconut sugar

- 1 tsp garlic powder

- 1 tsp onion powder

- 4 tbsp avocado oil

SAUTÉED PORK CHOPS

SERVING SIZE 4   TIME 30 MINUTES

DIRECTIONS

1.   Heat large cast-iron pan on the stove over medium heat until warm, about 5 minutes.

2.   While cast-iron pan is heating, sprinkle spices evenly over the pork chops. Make sure to get both sides of the meat on each pork chop.

3.   Drizzle avocado oil into the warmed cast-iron pan, followed by the pork chops. Cook the pork chops until bottom side of the pork chops is golden brown, about 6 minutes.

4.   Using tongs, flip the pork chops to cook the opposite side. Continue cooking the pork chops until both sides of the pork chops are golden brown and the pork chops internal temperature read 145°F.

5.   Remove pork chops from heat; serve warm.

STORAGE

REFRIGERATOR Sautéed pork chops can be stored in the refrigerator for up to 1 week.

FREEZER Sautéed pork chops can be stored in the refrigerator for up to 1 month.

REHEATING INSTRUCTIONS

REFRIGERATOR Heat oven to 350°F. Prepare a baking tray by lining it with 1 sheet of parchment paper. Place pork chops on the prepared baking tray. Place baking tray in the oven and cook until pork chops are warm, about 7–10 minutes.

FREEZER Heat oven to 350°F. Prepare a baking tray by lining it with 1 sheet of parchment paper. Place pork chops on the prepared baking tray. Place baking tray in the oven and cook until pork chops are warm, about 18–25 minutes.

SEAFOOD

Fried Fish Fillets 63

Grilled Pineapple Shrimp. 65

Halibut 67

Oven-Roasted Mackerel 68

Dill Lemongrass Roasted Salmon 71

Scallops 73

Shrimp 75

Turbot 76

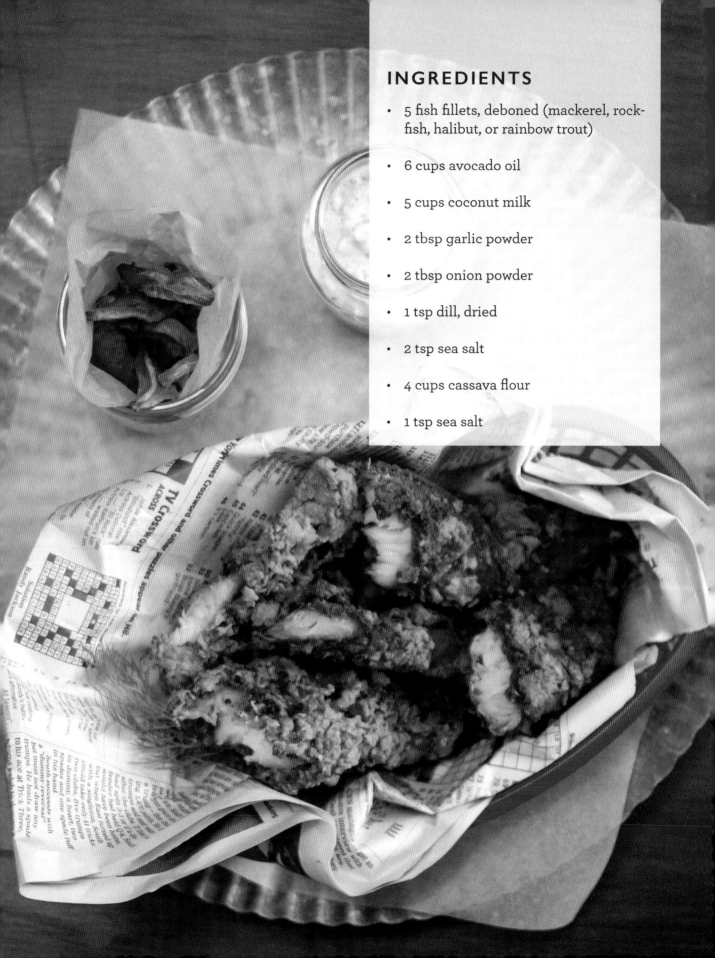

INGREDIENTS

- 5 fish fillets, deboned (mackerel, rock-fish, halibut, or rainbow trout)

- 6 cups avocado oil

- 5 cups coconut milk

- 2 tbsp garlic powder

- 2 tbsp onion powder

- 1 tsp dill, dried

- 2 tsp sea salt

- 4 cups cassava flour

- 1 tsp sea salt

FRIED FISH FILLETS

SERVING SIZE 5   TIME 1 HOUR

DIRECTIONS

1. Place the 6 cups of avocado oil in a large cast-iron pan over medium high heat on the stove. Heat the oil until a thermometer inserted into the oil reads 375°F.

2. Place the coconut milk, garlic powder, onion powder, dill, and 2 tsp of sea salt in a large bowl. Using a whisk, whisk the mixture together until the mixture is smooth, about 2 minutes.

3. Place the cassava flour and 1 tsp sea salt in a medium sized bowl. Using a whisk, whisk the ingredients together until fully combined, about 20 seconds.

4. To make the fish fillets, dip a fish fillet first in the coconut milk mixture and then in the cassava flour mixture.

5. Place the coated fish fillet in the heated oil. Repeat steps 4 and 5 until all fish fillets have been coated in both the coconut milk and cassava flour mixtures and placed in the heated oil to cook. Do not overcrowd the pan or the fish will not cook properly.

6. Cook fish until the side facing the bottom of the cast-iron pan turns golden brown, about 5 minutes. Flip fish fillets over and cook until the opposite side turns golden brown, about 4 minutes.

7. Once the fish fillets are done cooking, remove the fish fillets from the oil and place on a paper towels to drain off excess oil.

8. Serve warm.

STORAGE

FREEZER Fillets can be stored in the freezer for up to 2 months.

REHEATING INSTRUCTIONS

FREEZER Preheat oven to 350°F. Prepare a baking tray by lining it with a sheet of parchment paper. Place fish fillets on the prepared baking tray. Place the baking tray in the oven and cook until the fish fillets are warm, about 13 minutes.

INGREDIENTS

- 1 pound shrimp, shell still on

- 1 pineapple, skin removed, cut into large chunks about half the size of the shrimp

- 2 tbsp avocado oil

- 1 tsp sea salt

- 6 wooden skewers

GRILLED PINEAPPLE SHRIMP

SERVING SIZE **4**   TIME **30 MINUTES**

DIRECTIONS

1. Heat a grill to 300°F. If using coals, light coals on fire and burn until coals turn gray. Place the coals to the left side of the grill.

2. On the wooden skewers, skewer a piece of shrimp, followed by a piece of pineapple. Repeat this step until all shrimp and pineapple have been skewered.

3. Drizzle both sides of the shrimp and pineapple pieces with avocado oil.

4. Sprinkle both sides of the shrimp and pineapple pieces with sea salt.

5. Place the pineapple shrimp skewers on the grill. Cook the shrimp pineapple skewers until the shrimp have turned a bright orange pink color, about 20–25 minutes. If using coals, place the shrimp pineapple skewers on the right side of the grill, away from the coals. This will provide indirect heat to the skewers and prevent the shrimp and pineapple from burning.

6. Serve warm.

STORAGE

Grilled pineapple shrimp are best served immediately after cooking.

INGREDIENTS

- 4 halibut fillets, deboned

- 1 tsp sea salt

- 1 tsp onion powder

- 1 tsp garlic powder

- 4 tsp coconut oil

HALIBUT

SERVING SIZE 4   TIME 30 MINUTES

DIRECTIONS

1.   Place a cast-iron pan on the stove over medium heat.

2.   While the cast-iron pan is heating, prepare the halibut fillets by sprinkling the top and bottom of the fillets with salt, onion powder, and garlic powder.

3.   Once the cast-iron pan is hot, pour 1 tsp of the coconut oil in the cast-iron pan.

4.   Lay the halibut fillets skin side down in the coconut oil.

5.   Cook for the halibut fillets over medium heat until the skin on the fillets becomes golden brown, about 5 minutes.

6.   Flip the halibut fillets over in the cast-iron pan. Pour the remaining coconut oil into the cast-iron pan. Cook until halibut turns an opaque white color, about 7 minutes.

7.   Serve warm.

STORAGE

REFRIGERATOR Halibut can be stored in the refrigerator for up to 3 days.

REHEATING INSTRUCTIONS

REFRIGERATOR Place halibut in a large pot with a drizzle of water on the stove over low heat. Cook halibut until warm, about 4 minutes.

OVEN-ROASTED MACKEREL

SERVING SIZE 4   TIME 30 MINUTES

INGREDIENTS

- 4 mackerel fillets, deboned

- 1 tsp sea salt

- 2 tbsp avocado oil

- 2 garlic cloves

- ½ onion, chopped

- 1 tsp white balsamic vinegar

DIRECTIONS

1. Preheat oven to 350°F. Prepare a baking tray by lining it with 1 sheet of parchment paper.

2. Place the mackerel onto the prepared baking tray.

3. Place the sea salt, avocado oil, garlic cloves, onion, and white balsamic vinegar into a blender. Blend until smooth, about 3 minutes.

4. Spread the blended mixture on both sides of the mackerel fillets.

5. Place another sheet of parchment paper on top of the mackerel fillets.

6. Place the baking tray in the oven. Cook mackerel fillets until the fish feels slightly firm and the flesh of the fish turns a more solid white color, about 30 minutes.

STORAGE

REFRIGERATOR Oven-roasted mackerel fillets can be stored in the refrigerator for up to 3 days.

REHEATING INSTRUCTIONS

REFRIGERATOR Place the oven-roasted mackerel fillets in a large pot with a drizzle of water on the stove over low heat. Cook the mackerel fillets until warm, about 3 minutes.

INGREDIENTS

- 4 salmon fillets, wild caught, deboned

- 1 tsp dill, dried

- 1 yellow onion, thinly sliced

- 1 lemongrass stalk, sliced in half lengthwise

- ½ tsp sea salt

- ½ tsp coconut oil

DILL LEMONGRASS ROASTED SALMON

SERVING SIZE 4   TIME 30 MINUTES

DIRECTIONS

1. Heat oven to 325°F. Prepare a baking tray by lining it with parchment paper that extends 4 inches past each end of the baking tray.

2. Place the onion down on the left side of the prepared baking tray, followed by the lemongrass.

3. Place the salmon directly over the lemongrass. Drizzle the coconut oil over the top of the salmon. Sprinkle the sea salt and dill over the top of the salmon and massage into the salmon.

4. Fold the right side of the parchment paper over the salmon, and tuck the end of the parchment paper under the onions to create an envelope.

5. Place the baking tray in the oven. Bake the salmon until the salmon's center turns a pale opaque pink color, about 25 minutes.

6. Serve warm.

STORAGE

REFRIGERATOR Roasted dill lemongrass salmon can be stored in the refrigerator for up to 3 days.

REHEATING INSTRUCTIONS

REFRIGERATOR Once roasted dill lemongrass salmon has been placed in the refrigerator for storage, it is best served chilled.

INGREDIENTS

- ¼ cup avocado oil

- 1 pound scallops, tongues removed

- 1 tsp sea salt

SCALLOPS

SERVING SIZE 4   TIME 25 MINUTES

DIRECTIONS

1. Place a large cast-iron pan on the stove over medium-high heat. Heat until the cast-iron pan is hot. It is important that the cast-iron pan is hot so that the scallops can obtain a golden brown color on top without overcooking.

2. While the pan is heating, prepare the scallops by sprinkling the sea salt over both sides of the scallops.

3. Once the pan is hot, pour the avocado oil in the pan.

4. Lay enough scallops down in the pan.

5. Cook scallops for 2 minutes over medium heat.

6. Flip the scallops over. Cook until scallops are golden brown, about 3 minutes.

7. Serve warm.

STORAGE

Scallops are best served immediately after cooking.

INGREDIENTS

- ¼ cup avocado oil

- 1½ pound shrimp, deveined

- 1 tsp sea salt

SHRIMP

SERVING SIZE 4   TIME 20 MINUTES

DIRECTIONS

1. Place a large cast-iron pan on the stove over medium heat.

2. While the pan is heating, prepare the shrimp by sprinkling the sea salt over both sides of the shrimp.

3. Pour the avocado oil in the cast-iron pan.

4. Lay the shrimp down in the cast-iron pan. Cook the shrimp for 2 minutes over medium heat.

5. Flip the shrimp over. Cook the shrimp until it becomes bright orange, about 3 minutes.

6. Serve warm.

STORAGE

Shrimp is best served immediately after cooking.

TURBOT

SERVING SIZE 4   TIME 35 MINUTES

INGREDIENTS

- 4 turbot fillets, deboned

- 2 tsp avocado oil

- 1 tsp sea salt

- 1 tsp onion powder

- 1 tsp garlic powder

- 1 lemongrass stalk, cut in half down the center

DIRECTIONS

1. Preheat oven to 350°F. Prepare a baking tray by lining it with 1 sheet of parchment paper.

2. Place the lemongrass on the prepared baking tray.

3. Drizzle the turbot fillets with avocado oil. Sprinkle the sea salt, onion powder, and garlic powder over the tops and bottoms of the turbot fillets.

4. Place the turbot fillets over the lemongrass. Place a second sheet of parchment paper over top of the turbot fillets.

5. Place the turbot fillets in the oven. Cook the turbot fillets until the fillets turn white in color, about 25 minutes.

6. Serve warm.

STORAGE

REFRIGERATOR Turbot fillets can be stored in the refrigerator for up to 3 days.

REHEATING INSTRUCTIONS

REFRIGERATOR Place turbot fillets in a large cast-iron pan with a drizzle of water. Place the cast-iron pan on the stove over low heat. Cook turbot fillets until warm, about 4 minutes.

VEGETABLES

Apple Strawberry Salad .80

Rainbow Carrot Salad 81

Artichokes 83

Asparagus 85

Bacon Brussels Sprouts 87

Beet Blueberry Salad. 89

Carrot Turmeric Puree 90

Cauliflower Rice 93

Honey Dill Carrots 95

Oven-Roasted Cauliflower 96

Parsnip Puree 99

Pesto Zucchini Salad 101

Pickled Thai Turmeric Cucumbers 103

Roasted Spaghetti Squash 105

Tzatziki Cucumbers 107

Vegetable Noodles .108

INGREDIENTS

- 4 artichokes

- 6 cups water

- 1 tbsp avocado oil

- 1 tsp sea salt

ARTICHOKES

SERVING SIZE 4   TIME 1 HOUR

DIRECTIONS

1. Using your hands, remove any smaller leaves toward the bottom of the artichokes. Using a pair of scissors, cut the tips off of the artichoke leaves.

2. Using a knife, slice the top 1/2 inch off the artichokes and 1 inch off the stem at the bottom of the artichokes.

3. Place the 6 cups of water and artichokes into a large pot on the stove over high heat and bring to a boil, about 10 minutes. Cook until leaves have become soft, about 40 minutes.

4. Remove the artichokes from the boiling water and slice down the center.

5. Drizzle each half of the artichokes with avocado oil and sprinkle with sea salt.

6. Serve warm.

STORAGE

REFRIGERATOR Artichokes can be kept in the refrigerator for up to 2 days.

REHEATING INSTRUCTIONS

REFRIGERATOR Place artichokes in a medium-sized pot with a drizzle of oil on the stove over medium-low heat. Heat until artichokes are warm, about 3 minutes.

INGREDIENTS

- 1 bunch asparagus, bottoms cut off; if the stalks are thick, peel off the bottom half of the skin

- coconut oil spray

- 1 tsp sea salt

ASPARAGUS

SERVING SIZE 4   TIME 20 MINUTES

DIRECTIONS

1. Heat the oven to 350°F. Prepare a baking tray by lining it with 1 sheet of parchment paper.

2. Lay asparagus down on the prepared sheet.

3. Lightly spray the asparagus with coconut oil spray and sprinkle the sea salt over the asparagus.

4. Place the baking tray in the oven and bake until asparagus is soft and shriveled up slightly, about 10–15 minutes.

5. Serve warm.

STORAGE

REFRIGERATOR Asparagus can be kept in the refrigerator for up to 1 week.

REHEATING INSTRUCTIONS

REFRIGERATOR Place asparagus in a medium-sized pot on the stove over low heat. Heat until warm, about 4 minutes.

INGREDIENTS

- ½ pound bacon

- 1 pound brussels sprouts, with ends off, cut in half

BACON BRUSSELS SPROUTS

SERVING SIZE 4   TIME 30 MINUTES

DIRECTIONS

1. Place bacon in a large cast-iron pan on the stove over medium-low heat. Cook bacon until crispy, about 7 minutes. Remove bacon from pan, let dry on paper towels, and allow to cool completely. This will allow the excess grease to be removed. Keep the bacon grease in the cast-iron pan.

2. Add brussels sprouts to the cast-iron pan and cook over medium heat until brussels sprouts are soft, about 7 minutes. Remove from pan.

3. While brussels sprouts are cooking, chop bacon into tiny little crumble pieces.

4. Top brussels sprouts with bacon crumbles.

5. Serve warm.

STORAGE

REFRIGERATOR Bacon brussels sprouts can be stored in the refrigerator for up to 1 week.

FREEZER Bacon brussels sprouts can be stored in the freezer for up to 3 months.

REHEATING INSTRUCTIONS

REFRIGERATOR Preheat oven to 350°F. Prepare a sheet tray by lining it with parchment paper. Place bacon brussels sprouts on the prepared baking tray and baking the oven until warm, about 5–7 minutes.

FREEZER Preheat oven to 350°F. Prepare a sheet tray by lining it with parchment paper. Place bacon brussels sprouts on the prepared baking tray and bake until warm, about 10–15 minutes.

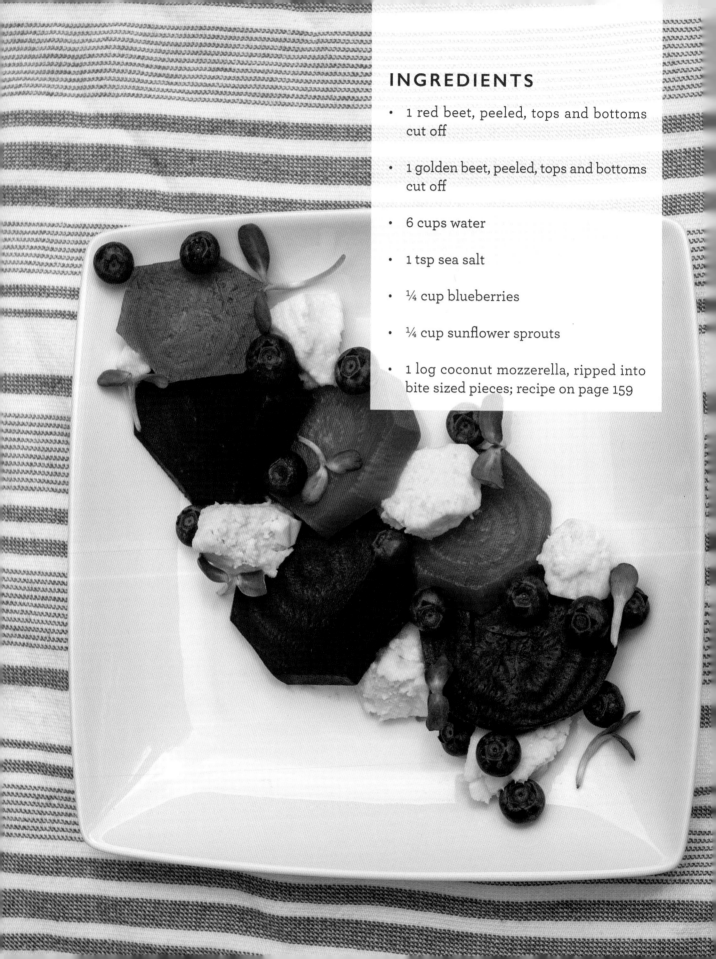

INGREDIENTS

- 1 red beet, peeled, tops and bottoms cut off

- 1 golden beet, peeled, tops and bottoms cut off

- 6 cups water

- 1 tsp sea salt

- ¼ cup blueberries

- ¼ cup sunflower sprouts

- 1 log coconut mozzerella, ripped into bite sized pieces; recipe on page 159

BEET BLUEBERRY SALAD

SERVING SIZE 4   TIME 45 MINUTES

DIRECTIONS

1. Place the 6 cups of water and sea salt into a large pot on the stove over high heat and bring to a boil, about 10 minutes.

2. Add the red and golden beets to the boiling water and cook until fork-tender, about 40 minutes.

3. Remove the beets from the boiling water; discard the water. Allow the beets to cool completely.

4. Slice the beets into thick slices and arrange in a line on a plate.

5. Top the beets with the coconut milk cheese, blueberries, and sunflower sprouts.

6. Serve cold or at room temperature.

STORAGE

REFRIGERATOR Beet blueberry salad can be kept in the refrigerator for up to 2 days.

CARROT TURMERIC PUREE

SERVING SIZE 4   TIME 45 MINUTES

INGREDIENTS

- ¾ pound carrots, peeled, tops removed, roughly chopped

- 6 cups water

- 3 cups mother sauce; recipe on page 136

- 2 tbsp turmeric, dried, ground

- ½ tsp sea salt

DIRECTIONS

1. Place the water in a large pot on the stove over high heat and bring to a boil, about 10 minutes.

2. Add the carrots to the boiling water and cook until fork-tender, about 20 minutes. Discard the water.

3. Place the carrots, mother sauce, turmeric, and sea salt in a blender. Blend until smooth, about 5 minutes.

4. Place pureed mixture in a medium-sized pot on the stove and heat over low until warm, about 3 minutes.

5. Serve warm.

STORAGE

REFRIGERATOR Carrot turmeric puree can be stored in the refrigerator for up to 2 weeks.

FREEZER Carrot turmeric puree sauce can be stored in the freezer for up to 2 months.

REHEATING INSTRUCTIONS

REFRIGERATOR Place carrot turmeric puree in a medium-sized pot. Place the pot on the stove over medium-low heat. Heat until warm, about 4 minutes.

FREEZER Place carrot turmeric puree in a medium-sized pot. Place the pot on the stove over medium-low heat. Heat until warm, about 10 minutes.

INGREDIENTS

- 1 package (12oz) riced cauliflower

- 1 yellow onion, diced

- 1 garlic clove, diced

- 1 tsp sea salt

- 1 tbsp onion powder

- 2 tsp garlic powder

- 2 tbsp avocado oil

- ¼ cup water

CAULIFLOWER RICE

SERVING SIZE 4   TIME 30 MINUTES

DIRECTIONS

1.   Place a medium-sized cast-iron pan on the stove over medium heat until warm, about 5 minutes.

2.   Add the avocado oil, diced onion, sea salt, and garlic to the heated pan. Cook over medium-low heat until onions are golden brown, about 4 minutes, stirring occasionally with a wooden spoon.

3.   Add the riced cauliflower, onion powder, garlic powder, and water to the cast-iron pan. Cook until the riced cauliflower is hot and soft, about 5 minutes, stirring occasionally with a wooden spoon. Do not overcook the mixture or the riced cauliflower will become mushy.

4.   Serve warm.

STORAGE

REFRIGERATOR Cauliflower rice can be stored in the refrigerator for up to 2 weeks.

FREEZER Cauliflower rice can be stored in the freezer for up to 2 months.

REHEATING INSTRUCTIONS

REFRIGERATOR Place cauliflower rice and a drizzle of water in a medium-sized pot. Place the pot on the stove over medium-low heat. Heat until warm, about 4 minutes.

FREEZER Place cauliflower rice and a drizzle of water in a medium-sized pot. Place the pot on the stove over medium-low heat. Heat until warm, about 10 minutes.

INGREDIENTS

- 1 pound carrots, peeled, tops and bottoms trimmed

- ¼ cup water

- 1 tbsp honey, raw

- 2 tsp dill, fresh, chopped

- 1 tsp sea salt

- 2 tbsp avocado oil

- 1 tbsp apple cider vinegar

- 1 tsp garlic powder

HONEY DILL CARROTS

SERVING SIZE 4   TIME 30 MINUTES

DIRECTIONS

1. Heat oven to 350°F. Prepare a baking tray by lining it with 1 sheet of parchment paper.

2. In a small bowl, whisk together the water, honey, dill, sea salt, avocado oil, apple cider vinegar, and garlic powder.

3. Place the carrots on the prepared baking tray. Pour the water and honey mixture over the carrots.

4. Cover the top of the carrots with another piece of parchment paper.

5. Place the baking tray in the oven and cook until carrots are fork-tender, about 30 minutes.

6. Serve warm.

STORAGE

REFRIGERATOR Honey dill carrots can be stored in the refrigerator for up to 1 week.

FREEZER Honey dill carrots can be stored in the freezer for up to 2 months.

REHEATING INSTRUCTIONS

REFRIGERATOR Place honey dill carrots and a drizzle of water in a medium-sized pot. Place the pot on the stove over medium-low heat. Heat until warm, about 4 minutes.

FREEZER Place honey dill carrots and a drizzle of water in a medium-sized pot. Place the pot on the stove over medium-low heat. Heat until warm, about 10 minutes.

INGREDIENTS

- 2 zucchinis, tops and bottoms trimmed

- 1 cup pesto; recipe on page 141

- 1 tsp apple cider vinegar

PESTO ZUCCHINI SALAD

SERVING SIZE 4   TIME 5 MINUTES

DIRECTIONS

1. Using a vegetable peeler, peel the zucchini into thin ribbons.

2. Place zucchini ribbons, pesto, and apple cider vinegar into a large bowl. Toss zucchini ribbons with pesto and apple cider vinegar until ribbons are evenly coated.

3. Serve cold or at room temperature.

STORAGE

REFRIGERATOR Pesto zucchini salad can be kept in the refrigerator for up to 1 week.

INGREDIENTS

- 1 cucumber, sliced thin

- 1 cup coconut milk, from a can

- 1½ tsp sea salt

- 1 tsp turmeric powder

- ½ tsp onion powder

- ¼ tsp garlic powder

- 1½ tsp dill, dried or fresh

- 2 tsp coconut sugar

- ½ cup balsamic vinegar

PICKLED THAI TURMERIC CUCUMBERS

SERVING SIZE 4   TIME I HOUR I0 MINUTES

DIRECTIONS

1. Whisk all ingredients together in a large bowl, with the exception of the cucumbers, until fully combined, about 2 minutes.

2. Add cucumbers to the bowl. Toss cucumbers in the coconut milk mixture, making sure each cucumber slice is coated fully, about 2 minutes.

3. Allow mixture to sit in the refrigerator for 1 hour to let the flavors marinate into the cucumber slices.

4. Serve cold or at room temperature.

STORAGE

REFRIGERATOR Pickled Thai turmeric cucumbers can be kept in the refrigerator for up to 3 weeks.

INGREDIENTS

- 1 spaghetti squash, cut in half, deseeded

- 2 tbsp avocado oil

- 2 tsp sea salt

ROASTED SPAGHETTI SQUASH

SERVING SIZE 4 AS A SIDE, 2 AS A MAIN DISH   TIME 45 MINUTES

DIRECTIONS

1.   Heat oven to 425°F. Prepare a baking tray by lining it with 1 sheet of parchment paper.

2.   Place spaghetti squash on the prepared baking tray, flesh side up. Drizzle each top of spaghetti squash with 1 tbsp of avocado oil. Sprinkle the sea salt over the 2 squash halves.

3.   Flip the squash over so the skin side faces upward. Place the baking tray in the oven and cook until squash skin is brown and center gives away easily, about 25–30 minutes.

4.   To serve, scrape out center of squash and serve warm.

     OPTIONAL MAIN DISH ADDITIONS   Scrape out center of squash. Add meat of your choosing, such as roasted chicken breast. Toss together and place back in the skin. Cook in the oven until meat is hot.

STORAGE

REFRIGERATOR Roasted spaghetti squash can be stored in the refrigerator for up to 2 weeks.

FREEZER Roasted spaghetti squash can be stored in the freezer for up to 2 months.

REHEATING INSTRUCTIONS

REFRIGERATOR Place roasted spaghetti squash and a drizzle of water in a medium-sized pot. Place the pot on the stove over medium-low heat. Heat until warm, about 4 minutes.

FREEZER Place roasted spaghetti squash and a drizzle of water in a medium-sized pot. Place the pot on the stove over medium-low heat. Heat until warm, about 10 minutes.

INGREDIENTS

- 2 cups coconut milk, from a can

- 2 tsp dill, dried

- ¼ tsp sea salt

- 2 tsp onion powder

- 1 tsp garlic powder

- 1 tsp white balsamic vinegar

- 2 cucumbers, sliced thinly

TZATZIKI CUCUMBERS

SERVING SIZE 4   TIME 1 HOUR 10 MINUTES

DIRECTIONS

1. Place all ingredients, with the exception of the cucumbers, in a blender. Blend until smooth, about 2 minutes.

2. Place cucumbers in a large bowl. Pour the blended mixture over the cucumbers and toss until cucumbers are evenly coated, about 2 minutes.

3. Allow the cucumbers and blended mixture to marinate for about an hour in the refrigerator.

4. Serve cold or at room temperature.

STORAGE

REFRIGERATOR Tzatziki cucumbers can be kept in the refrigerator for up to 3 weeks.

VEGETABLE NOODLES

SERVING SIZE **4**   TIME **20 MINUTES**

INGREDIENTS

- 1 pound vegetable noodles (beet, zucchini, or carrot work well)

- 4 tsp avocado oil

- 1 tsp sea salt

- 1 tsp onion powder

- 1 tsp garlic powder

- 2 tsp water

DIRECTIONS

1. Place a cast-iron pan on the stove over medium heat until warm, about 5 minutes.

2. Once the cast-iron pan is warm, add the vegetable noodles, avocado oil, sea salt, and water. Cook over medium heat until noodles are soft, about 4 minutes.

3. Add the onion powder and garlic powder to the cast-iron pan. Using a wooden spoon, stir the spices into the vegetable noodles until evenly coated, about 1 minute. Cook over low heat for 5 minutes.

4. Serve warm.

STORAGE

REFRIGERATOR Vegetable noodles can be stored in the refrigerator for up to 1 week.

FREEZER Vegetable noodles can be stored in the freezer for up to 2 months.

REHEATING INSTRUCTIONS

REFRIGERATOR Place vegetable noodles and a drizzle of water in a medium-sized pot. Place the pot on the stove over medium-low heat. Heat until warm, about 4 minutes.

FREEZER Place vegetable noodles and a drizzle of water in a medium-sized pot. Place the pot on the stove over medium-low heat. Heat until warm, about 10 minutes.

SAUCES, DRESSINGS, SEASONINGS

Alfredo Sauce 112

Apple Rosemary Sauce 115

Blackberry Sauce 117

Chicken, Turkey, or Pork Roast Brine 118

Creamy Onion Sauce 119

Caramelized Onion Curry Sauce 121

Creamy Mushroom Sauce .123

Creamy Spinach Sauce 125

French Onion Sauce 126

Herbs de Provence Sauce .129

Italian Dressing 130

Roasted Garlic Coconut Glaze 131

"Ketchup" 133

Korean Barbecue Sauce 135

Mother Sauce 136

Ginger Peach Sauce 138

Pesto 141

Pineapple Parsley Sauce .142

Ranch Dressing 145

Sweet and Sour Sauce 146

Tartar Sauce 148

Curry Seasoning 149

"Tomato" Sauce 151

ALFREDO SAUCE

SERVING SIZE 2 CUPS   TIME 30 MINUTES

INGREDIENTS

- 1 head cauliflower, leaves and center stem removed, chopped into 1-inch-thick pieces

- 6 cups water

- 1 cup coconut cream

- ¼ cup water

- 2 tbsp tapioca flour or tapioca starch

- ½ tbsp apple cider vinegar

- ½ tsp sea salt

- ¼ tsp garlic powder

DIRECTIONS

1. Place the 6 cups of water into a large pot. Place the pot of water on the stove over high heat and bring to a boil, about 10 minutes.

2. Add the cauliflower to the pot of boiling water. Bring the water back to a boil and continue to cook the cauliflower until fork-tender, about 4 minutes.

3. Once cauliflower is fork-tender, remove the cauliflower from the boiling water; discard the water.

4. Place the cauliflower and remaining ingredients in a blender and blend until smooth, about 5 minutes.

5. Serve warm; enjoy!

STORAGE

REFRIGERATOR Alfredo sauce can be stored in the refrigerator for up to 1 week.

FREEZER Alfredo sauce can be stored in the freezer for up to 2 months.

REHEATING INSTRUCTIONS

REFRIGERATOR Place alfredo sauce in a medium-sized pot. Place the pot on the stove over medium-low heat and heat until warm, about 4 minutes.

FREEZER Place alfredo sauce in a medium-sized pot. Place the pot on the stove over medium-low heat and heat until warm, about 4 minutes.

INGREDIENTS

- 1 yellow onion, diced

- 2 tbsp avocado oil

- sprinkle sea salt

- 1 tsp rosemary, dried

- 3 apples, cored, cut into 1-inch-thick slices

- 1 cup apple juice, no sugar added, not from concentrate

APPLE ROSEMARY SAUCE

SERVING SIZE 2 CUPS   TIME 30 MINUTES

DIRECTIONS

1. Place a medium-sized cast-iron pan on the stove over medium heat. Heat until warm, about 4 minutes.

2. Add the avocado oil and diced onions to the warmed pan. Cook the onions until translucent, stirring occasionally with a wooden spoon, about 5 minutes.

3. Add the sea salt, rosemary, apple juice, and apples to the onions. Turn heat up on the stove up to medium high heat and bring mixture to a boil.

4. Once mixture has come to boil, reduce heat to low and simmer for 10 minutes.

5. Once the mixture has simmered for 10 minutes, place the entire mixture, apples included, in a blender. Blend until smooth, about 3 minutes.

6. Serve warm.

7. Sauce can be strained for a smoother consistency if desired.

STORAGE

REFRIGERATOR Apple rosemary sauce can be stored in the refrigerator for up to 2 weeks.

FREEZER Apple rosemary sauce can be stored in the freezer for up to 2 months.

REHEATING INSTRUCTIONS

REFRIGERATOR Place apple rosemary sauce in a medium-sized pot. Place the pot on the stove over medium-low heat. Heat until warm, about 4 minutes.

FREEZER Place apple rosemary sauce in a medium-sized pot. Place the pot on the stove over medium-low heat. Heat until warm, about 10 minutes.

INGREDIENTS

- 2 pints blackberries

- 1 yellow onion, diced

- 1 cup pomegranate juice, no sugar added, not from concentrate

- 2 tbsp white balsamic vinegar

- 2 tbsp avocado oil

BLACKBERRY SAUCE

SERVING SIZE 1 CUP   TIME 30 MINUTES

DIRECTIONS

1. Place a medium-sized cast-iron pan on the stove over medium heat. Heat cast-iron pan until warm, about 4 minutes.

2. Add the avocado oil and diced onions to the warm cast-iron pan. Cook over medium heat until onions are translucent, stirring occasionally with a wooden spoon, about 4 minutes.

3. Add the blackberries and white balsamic vinegar to the cast-iron pan. Cook over low heat until blackberries are soft, about 5 minutes.

4. Add the pomegranate juice to the cast-iron pan and simmer over low heat for 5 minutes.

5. Once sauce has simmered for 5 minutes, place all ingredients into a blender and blend the sauce until smooth, about 3 minutes.

6. Once the sauce has been blended until smooth, strain the sauce through a fine mesh sieve to remove blackberry seeds.

7. Sauce can be served warm or cold.

STORAGE

REFRIGERATOR Blackberry sauce can be stored in the refrigerator for up to 2 weeks.

FREEZER Blackberry sauce can be stored in the freezer for up to 2 months.

REHEATING INSTRUCTIONS

REFRIGERATOR Place blackberry sauce in a medium-sized pot. Place the pot on the stove over medium-low heat. Heat until warm, about 4 minutes.

FREEZER Place blackberry sauce in a medium-sized pot. Place the pot on the stove over medium-low heat. Heat until warm, about 10 minutes.

CHICKEN, TURKEY, OR PORK ROAST BRINE

BRINE FOR ONE 15 LB. TURKEY, ONE WHOLE-BIRD CHICKEN, OR ONE 4 LB. PORK RIB ROAST

TIME 1 HOUR 30 MINUTES

INGREDIENTS

- 2 cups chicken, beef, or vegetable stock
- 4 cups water
- 1 cinnamon stick
- 2 cups sea salt
- ½ cup coconut sugar
- 2 apples, any variety, sliced thinly

- 2 rosemary springs, fresh
- 6 sage leaves
- 1 pomegranate, quartered
- 4 tarragon sprigs, fresh
- 6 thyme sprigs, fresh
- 3 bay leaves, dried or fresh

DIRECTIONS

1. Place all ingredients in a large pot and cover with a lid. Place pot on the stove and bring to a boil over high heat, about 15 minutes. Once the mixture has come to a boil, turn off the heat and remove the lid.

2. Allow the brine to cool completely before using; this can take about 1 hour.

STORAGE

REFRIGERATOR Brine can be stored in the refrigerator for up to 2 weeks.

CREAMY ONION SAUCE

SERVING SIZE **4 CUPS**   TIME **40 MINUTES**

INGREDIENTS

- 4 cups mother sauce; recipe on page 136

- 2 yellow onions, sliced thinly

- 4 tbsp avocado oil

- ½ tsp sea salt

DIRECTIONS

1. Place a cast-iron pan on the stove over medium heat and heat until warm, about 4 minutes.

2. Add the avocado oil, onions, and sea salt. Cook the onions, stirring occasionally with a wooden spoon, until golden brown, about 5 minutes.

3. Add mother sauce to the cast-iron pan. Using a wooden spoon, stir the mother sauce into the cooked onions. Raise heat on the stove to medium high and bring mixture to a boil, stirring occasionally with a wooden spoon, about 5 minutes.

4. Once mixture comes to a boil, turn down heat on the stove to low and let the sauce simmer for 10 minutes, stirring occasionally with a wooden spoon.

5. Serve warm.

STORAGE

REFRIGERATOR Creamy onion sauce can be stored in the refrigerator for up to 2 weeks.

FREEZER Creamy onion sauce can be stored in the freezer for up to 2 months.

REHEATING INSTRUCTIONS

REFRIGERATOR Place creamy onion sauce in a medium-sized pot. Place the pot on the stove over medium-low heat. Heat until warm, about 4 minutes.

FREEZER Place creamy onion sauce in a medium-sized pot. Place the pot on the stove over medium-low heat. Heat until warm, about 10 minutes.

INGREDIENTS

- 1 yellow onion, thinly sliced

- 2 tbsp avocado oil

- 2 cups coconut milk, from a can

- 1 tsp sea salt

- 2 tsp coconut sugar

- 1/2 tsp garlic powder

- 1 tbsp curry seasoning; recipe on page 149

OPTIONAL MIX-INS:

- 1 cup sautéed chicken; recipe on page 57

- boiled sweet potatoes, skin removed, cut into bite-sized pieces

- steamed cauliflower, leaves and core removed, cut into bite-sized pieces

CARAMELIZED ONION CURRY SAUCE

SERVING SIZE 4   TIME 1 HOUR

DIRECTIONS

1. Place a medium-sized cast-iron pan on the stove. Heat the cast-iron pan over medium heat until warm, about 4 minutes.

2. Add the diced onions and avocado oil to the warmed cast-iron pan. Cook onions until golden brown, stirring occasionally with a wooden spoon, about 10 minutes.

3. Add the coconut milk, sea salt, coconut sugar, garlic powder, and curry seasoning to the cast-iron pan. Raise the heat on the stove to medium high and bring the mixture to a simmer, stirring occasionally with a wooden spoon, for 35 minutes.

4. Pour caramelized onion curry sauce over optional mix-ins.

5. Serve warm.

STORAGE

REFRIGERATOR Caramelized onion curry sauce can be stored in the refrigerator for up to 2 weeks.

FREEZER Caramelized onion curry sauce can be stored in the freezer for up to 2 months.

REHEATING INSTRUCTIONS

REFRIGERATOR Place caramelized onion curry sauce in a medium-sized pot. Place the pot on the stove over medium-low heat. Heat until warm, about 4 minutes.

FREEZER Place caramelized onion curry sauce in a medium-sized pot. Place the pot on the stove over medium-low heat. Heat until warm, about 10 minutes.

INGREDIENTS

- 4 cups mother sauce; recipe on page 136

- 1 pound oyster mushrooms, sliced thin

- 2 tbsp avocado oil

- ½ tsp sea salt

CREAMY MUSHROOM SAUCE

SERVING SIZE 4 CUPS   TIME 35 MINUTES

DIRECTIONS

1.   Place a cast-iron pan on the stove over medium heat and heat until warm, about 4 minutes.

2.   Add the avocado oil, oyster mushrooms, and sea salt. Cook the mushrooms, stirring occasionally with a wooden spoon, until golden brown, about 5 minutes.

3.   Add mother sauce to the cast-iron pan. Using a wooden spoon, stir the mother sauce into the cooked oyster mushrooms. Raise heat on the stove to medium high and bring mixture to a boil, stirring occasionally with a wooden spoon, about 5 minutes.

4.   Once mixture comes to a boil, turn down heat on the stove to low and let the sauce simmer for 10 minutes, stirring occasionally with a wooden spoon.

5.   Serve warm.

STORAGE

REFRIGERATOR Creamy mushroom sauce can be stored in the refrigerator for up to 2 weeks.

FREEZER Creamy mushroom sauce can be stored in the freezer for up to 2 months.

REHEATING INSTRUCTIONS

REFRIGERATOR Place creamy mushroom sauce in a medium-sized pot. Place the pot on the stove over medium-low heat. Heat until warm, about 4 minutes.

FREEZER Place creamy mushroom sauce in a medium-sized pot. Place the pot on the stove over medium-low heat. Heat until warm, about 10 minutes.

INGREDIENTS

- 2 cups spinach leaves

- 1 tbsp avocado oil

- 4 cups mother sauce; recipe on page 136

- ½ tsp sea salt

CREAMY SPINACH SAUCE

SERVING SIZE **4 CUPS**   TIME **30 MINUTES**

DIRECTIONS

1.   Place a cast-iron pan on the stove over medium heat and heat until warm, about 4 minutes.

2.   Add the avocado oil, spinach leaves, and sea salt. Cook the spinach leaves, stirring occasionally with a wooden spoon, until wilted, about 3 minutes.

3.   Add mother sauce to the cast-iron pan. Using a wooden spoon, stir the mother sauce into the cooked spinach leaves. Raise heat on the stove to medium high and bring mixture to a boil, stirring occasionally with a wooden spoon, about 5 minutes.

4.   Once mixture comes to a boil, turn down heat on the stove to low and let the sauce simmer for 10 minutes, stirring occasionally with a wooden spoon.

5.   Serve warm.

STORAGE

REFRIGERATOR Creamy spinach sauce can be stored in the refrigerator for up to 2 weeks.

FREEZER Creamy spinach sauce can be stored in the freezer for up to 2 months.

REHEATING INSTRUCTIONS

REFRIGERATOR Place creamy spinach sauce in a medium-sized pot. Place the pot on the stove over medium-low heat. Heat until warm, about 4 minutes.

FREEZER Place creamy spinach sauce in a medium-sized pot. Place the pot on the stove over medium-low heat. Heat until warm, about 10 minutes.

FRENCH ONION SAUCE

SERVING SIZE 4 CUPS   TIME 35 MINUTES

INGREDIENTS

- 4 cups beef stock
- 2 yellow onions, thinly sliced
- 2 garlic cloves, diced
- 2 rosemary sprigs, fresh
- 3 tbsp avocado oil

DIRECTIONS

1. Place a medium-sized cast-iron pan on the stove over medium heat. Heat until warm, about 4 minutes.

2. Add the avocado oil, garlic, and diced onions to the warmed pan. Cook the garlic and onions until translucent, stirring occasionally with a wooden spoon, about 5 minutes.

3. Add the rosemary sprigs and beef stock to the cast-iron pan. Using a wooden spoon, stir the beef stock into the onions and garlic.

4. Turn the heat on the stove down to low and allow sauce to simmer for 20 minutes.

5. Serve warm.

STORAGE

REFRIGERATOR French onion sauce can be stored in the refrigerator for up to 2 weeks.

FREEZER French onion sauce can be stored in the freezer for up to 2 months.

REHEATING INSTRUCTIONS

REFRIGERATOR Place French onion sauce in a medium-sized pot. Place the pot on the stove over medium-low heat. Heat until warm, about 4 minutes.

FREEZER Place French onion sauce in a medium-sized pot. Place the pot on the stove over medium-low heat. Heat until warm, about 10 minutes.

INGREDIENTS

- 4 cups mother sauce; recipe on page 136

- 1 tbsp Herbs de Provence seasoning

- ½ tsp sea salt

HERBS DE PROVENCE SAUCE

SERVING SIZE 4 CUPS   TIME 35 MINUTES

DIRECTIONS

1.   Place mother sauce, Herbs de Provence, and sea salt in a large pot. Using a whisk, whisk ingredients together until smooth.

2.   Place the large pot on the stove over low heat.

3.   Cook the sauce on the stove over low heat until sauce is warm, about 10 minutes.

4.   Serve warm.

STORAGE

REFRIGERATOR Herbs de Provence sauce can be stored in the refrigerator for up to 2 weeks.

FREEZER Herbs de Provence sauce can be stored in the freezer for up to 2 months.

REHEATING INSTRUCTIONS

REFRIGERATOR Place Herbs de Provence sauce in a medium-sized pot. Place the pot on the stove over medium-low heat. Heat until warm, about 4 minutes.

FREEZER Place Herbs de Provence sauce in a medium-sized pot. Place the pot on the stove over medium-low heat. Heat until warm, about 10 minutes.

INGREDIENTS

- 6 cups water

- 1 pound carrots, peeled, chopped into roughly 1-inch pieces

- 2 large beets, peeled, chopped into roughly 1-inch pieces

- 4 tbsp coconut sugar

- ¼ cup white balsamic vinegar

- 1 tsp sea salt

- 2 tsp onion powder

- 1 tsp garlic powder

"KETCHUP"

SERVING SIZE 2 CUPS   TIME 1 HOUR

DIRECTIONS

1. Place water into a large pot. Place pot of water on the stove and bring water to a boil over high heat, about 10 minutes.

2. Place carrots and beets into the pot of boiling water. Bring water back to a boil and continue to cook carrots and beets until fork-tender, about 20 minutes.

3. Once carrots and beets are fork-tender, remove them from the boiling water; discard the water. Place carrots, beets, and remaining ingredients into a blender. Blend all ingredients until smooth, about 5 minutes.

4. Place the blended mixture into a medium-sized pot. Place the pot on the stove over medium-low heat and bring to a simmer, about 5 minutes.

5. Continue to cook the blended mixture over medium-low heat for 20 minutes, stirring occasionally with a wooden spoon to prevent mixture from sticking to the bottom of the pot and burning.

6. Once blended mixture has cooked for 20 minutes on medium-low heat, remove pot from heat and allow blended mixture to cool at room temperature until mixture reaches room temperature, about 30 minutes.

7. Serve cold.

STORAGE

REFRIGERATOR "Ketchup" can be stored in the refrigerator for up to 3 months.

INGREDIENTS

- ¼ cup sesame oil

- 1 yellow onion, chopped

- 2 garlic cloves

- 3 tbsp coconut aminos

- ⅛ tsp sea salt

- 2 tbsp white balsamic vinegar

- 2 tsp coconut sugar

KOREAN BARBECUE SAUCE

SERVING SIZE 1 CUP   TIME 30 MINUTES

DIRECTIONS

1.   Place all ingredients in a blender. Blend until smooth, about 4 minutes.

2.   Sauce can be served cold or brushed over warm meat or fish.

STORAGE

REFRIGERATOR Korean barbecue sauce can be stored in the refrigerator for up to 2 weeks.

FREEZER Korean barbecue sauce can be stored in the freezer for up to 2 months.

REHEATING INSTRUCTIONS

REFRIGERATOR Place Korean barbecue sauce in a medium-sized pot. Place the pot on the stove over medium-low heat. Heat until warm, about 4 minutes.

FREEZER Place Korean barbecue sauce in a medium-sized pot. Place the pot on the stove over medium-low heat. Heat until warm, about 10 minutes.

MOTHER SAUCE

SERVING SIZE 6 CUPS   TIME 35 MINUTES

INGREDIENTS

- 8 cups coconut milk, from a can

- 5 yellow onions, thinly sliced

- 5 garlic cloves, small diced

- 4 tbsp avocado oil

- 2 tbsp sea salt

- 2 tbsp onion powder

- 2 tbsp garlic powder

DIRECTIONS

1.   Place a large cast-iron pan on the stove over medium heat. Heat until warm.

2.   Add the avocado oil and onions to heated pan and cook until onions are translucent, about 4 minutes.

3.   Add the garlic to the onions and cook until onions and garlic are golden brown, about 4 minutes.

4.   Add the coconut milk to the onion and garlic mixture. Using a whisk, whisk the coconut milk into the onions and garlic.

5.   Lower heat on the stove to low. Cook the coconut milk, onion, and garlic mixture over low heat for 10 minutes.

6. Add the sea salt, onion powder, and garlic powder to the coconut milk mixture. Using a whisk, whisk salt and spices into the coconut milk. Continue to cook the mixture for an additional 10 minutes over low heat.

7. Serve warm.

STORAGE

REFRIGERATOR Mother sauce can be stored in the refrigerator for up to 2 weeks.

FREEZER Mother sauce can be stored in the freezer for up to 2 months.

REHEATING INSTRUCTIONS

REFRIGERATOR Place mother sauce in a medium-sized pot. Place the pot on the stove over medium-low heat. Heat until warm, about 4 minutes.

FREEZER Place mother sauce in a medium-sized pot. Place the pot on the stove over medium-low heat. Heat until warm, about 10 minutes.

*Coconut milk will solidify in the freezer and refrigerator, so do not worry if you see a thick layer of white after storage. It will remelt and liquify once reheated.

GINGER PEACH SAUCE

SERVING SIZE 2 CUPS   TIME 30 MINUTES

INGREDIENTS

- 2 peaches, skin removed, small diced

- 2 peaches, pureed, strained through a fine mesh sieve

- 2 red onions, diced

- 2 garlic cloves, diced

- 2 tbsp avocado oil

- 1 tbsp ginger, dried, ground

- ¼ cup apple juice, no sugar added, not from concentrate

- 2 tbsp white balsamic vinegar

- 2 tbsp coconut sugar

- 2 tbsp water

DIRECTIONS

1. Place a medium-sized cast-iron pan on the stove over medium heat. Heat until warm, about 4 minutes.

2. Add the avocado oil and diced onions to the warmed pan. Cook the onions until translucent, stirring occasionally with a wooden spoon, about 5 minutes.

3. Add the garlic and vinegar to the cast-iron pan. Cook the mixture over medium heat for 2 minutes.

4. Add the ginger, pureed peaches, and apple juice. Whisk together until fully combined. Continue to cook over low heat for 10 minutes.

5. While the mixture is cooking, place a separate medium-sized cast-iron pan on the stove over medium heat. Heat until warm, about 4 minutes.

6. Place the coconut sugar and water in the heated pan. Cook the sugar and water until the mixture comes to a boil, about 5 minutes.

7. Once the coconut sugar and water mixture comes to a boil, add the diced peaches to the pan. Using a wooden spoon, stir the peaches into the sugar and water mixture. Continue to cook the peaches over medium heat until they become soft and slightly golden brown, about 5 minutes.

8. Once the peaches become soft and slightly golden brown, add the peaches to the cast-iron pan containing the ginger, apple juice, and pureed peaches. Using a wooden spoon, stir the cooked peaches into the ginger and apple juice mixture. Continue cooking over medium heat for 2 minutes.

9. Serve warm.

STORAGE

REFRIGERATOR Peach ginger sauce can be stored in the refrigerator for up to 1 week.

FREEZER Peach ginger sauce can be stored in the freezer for up to 2 months.

REHEATING INSTRUCTIONS

REFRIGERATOR Place peach ginger sauce in a medium-sized pot. Place the pot on the stove over medium-low heat. Heat until warm, about 4 minutes.

FREEZER Place peach ginger sauce in a medium-sized pot. Place the pot on the stove over medium-low heat. Heat until warm, about 10 minutes.

INGREDIENTS

- 1 cup basil leaves, fresh

- ¼ cup avocado oil

- ¼ tsp sea salt

- 1 garlic clove

- 6 cups spinach leaves

- 1 tsp white balsamic vinegar

PESTO

SERVING SIZE 2 CUPS   TIME 10 MINUTES

DIRECTIONS

1.   Place all ingredients in a blender. Blend until smooth, about 4 minutes.

2.   Serve cold or at room temperature.

STORAGE

REFRIGERATOR Pesto can be stored in the refrigerator for up to 1 month.

PINEAPPLE PARSLEY SAUCE

SERVING SIZE 3 CUPS   TIME 40 MINUTES

INGREDIENTS

- 1 20 oz. can crushed pineapple

- 1 yellow onion, diced

- 2 tbsp avocado oil

- 2 tbsp coconut aminos

- 1 large pinch sea salt

- ¼ cup maple syrup

- 3 tbsp apple cider vinegar

- ¼ cup parsley, chopped finely

- ½ tbsp tapioca flour or tapioca starch

- 2 tbsp water

DIRECTIONS

1. Place a medium-sized cast-iron pan on the stove over medium heat. Heat until warm, about 4 minutes.

2. Add the avocado oil and diced onions to the warmed pan. Cook the onions until translucent, stirring occasionally with a wooden spoon, about 5 minutes.

3. Add the coconut aminos, apple cider vinegar, and sea salt to the pan. Raise heat on the stove to medium high and bring mixture to a simmer. Cook mixture for 12 minutes.

4. Add the maple syrup to the pan. Allow mixture to continue to simmer, stirring occasionally with a wooden spoon, for 4 minutes.

5. Add the crushed pineapple and parsley to the pan. Allow mixture to continue to simmer, stirring occasionally with a wooden spoon, for 15 minutes. Remove pan from heat.

6. Place pineapple and onion mixture into a blender. Blend until smooth, about 3 minutes. Pour mixture back into the pan.

7. In a separate bowl, using a whisk, whisk the tapioca flour or tapioca starch and water together to form a paste, about 30 seconds.

8. Using a whisk, whisk tapioca and water paste into the pineapple mixture.

9. Place the pan back on the stove over high heat. Bring mixture to a boil, whisking occasionally with a whisk, about 5 minutes.

10. Allow mixture to boil for 1 minute. Remove from heat.

11. Serve warm or cold.

STORAGE

REFRIGERATOR Pineapple parsley sauce can be stored in the refrigerator for up to 2 weeks.

FREEZER Pineapple parsley sauce can be stored in the freezer for up to 2 months.

REHEATING INSTRUCTIONS

REFRIGERATOR Place pineapple parsley sauce in a medium-sized pot. Place the pot on the stove over medium-low heat. Heat until warm, about 4 minutes.

FREEZER Place pineapple parsley sauce in a medium-sized pot. Place the pot on the stove over medium-low heat. Heat until warm, about 10 minutes.

INGREDIENTS

- 1 cup coconut milk, from a can

- 2 tbsp white balsamic vinegar

- ½ garlic clove

- 1 tbsp yellow onion, chopped

- 1 tbsp chives, fresh, diced

- 1 tbsp parsley, fresh, chopped

- 1 tbsp dill, dried

RANCH DRESSING

SERVING SIZE 1½ CUPS   TIME 10 MINUTES

DIRECTIONS

1.   Combine all ingredients in a blender. Blend until smooth, about 3 minutes.

2.   Serve cold.

STORAGE

REFRIGERATOR Ranch dressing can be stored in the refrigerator for up to 1 month.

SWEET AND SOUR SAUCE

SERVING SIZE 2 CUPS   TIME 30 MINUTES

INGREDIENTS

- ⅛ tsp ginger, fresh, grated

- 2 tbsp coconut aminos

- 1 ¼ cup pomegranate juice

- 3 tbsp white balsamic vinegar

- 2 tbsp water

- 1 ½ tbsp tapioca flour or tapioca starch

- 1 yellow onion, diced

- 2 garlic cloves, minced

- 1 tbsp coconut oil

- 2 ½ tbsp coconut sugar

- 2 pinches sea salt

DIRECTIONS

1. Place a medium-sized cast-iron pan on the stove over medium heat. Heat until warm, about 4 minutes.

2. Add the avocado oil and diced onions to the warmed cast-iron pan. Cook the onions until translucent, stirring occasionally with a wooden spoon, about 5 minutes.

3. Add in the garlic, sea salt, and ginger to the cast-iron pan, stirring occasionally with a wooden spoon until the garlic becomes golden brown, about 3 minutes.

4. Add in the white balsamic vinegar and coconut sugar to the cast-iron pan. Cook until vinegar is almost fully evaporated, stirring occasionally with a wooden spoon, about 3 minutes.

5. Pour the pomegranate juice into the cast-iron pan. Allow pomegranate juice to come to a simmer. Cook at a simmer for 15 minutes.

6. In a separate small bowl, using a whisk, whisk together the tapioca flour or tapioca starch and water to create a paste, about 30 seconds.

7.   Once mixture has simmered for 15 minutes, using a whisk, whisk the tapioca paste into the cast-iron pan to thicken the sauce. Allow to simmer for 5 additional minutes to cook out tapioca flavor.

8.   Remove pan from heat.

9.   Serve warm.

STORAGE

REFRIGERATOR Sweet and sour sauce can be stored in the refrigerator for up to 2 weeks.

FREEZER Sweet and sour sauce can be stored in the freezer for up to 2 months.

REHEATING INSTRUCTIONS

REFRIGERATOR Place sweet and sour sauce in a medium-sized pot. Place the pot on the stove over low heat. Heat until warm, about 4 minutes.

FREEZER Place sweet and sour sauce in a medium-sized pot. Place the pot on the stove over low heat. Heat until warm, about 10 minutes.

TARTAR SAUCE

SERVING SIZE 2 CUPS   TIME 10 MINUTES

INGREDIENTS

- 2 cups coconut milk, from a can

- 3 kosher baby dill pickles

- ½ cup white balsamic vinegar

- 2 sprigs dill, fresh or 1 tbsp dill, dried

DIRECTIONS

1. Place all ingredients in a blender.

2. Blend until smooth, about 5 minutes.

3. Serve cold.

STORAGE

REFRIGERATOR Tartar sauce can be stored in the refrigerator for up to 4 weeks.

CURRY SEASONING

SERVING SIZE ¼ CUP   TIME 10 MINUTES

INGREDIENTS

- 2 tbsp coriander, dried, ground

- 2 tbsp cumin, dried, ground

- 1½ tbsp turmeric, dried, ground

- 2 tsp ginger, dried, ground

- 1 tsp cinnamon, dried, ground

- ½ tsp cardamom, dried, ground

DIRECTIONS

1.   Whisk all ingredients together in a bowl.

2.   Place in an airtight container.

STORAGE

ROOM TEMPERATURE Keep curry seasoning stored in an airtight container at room temperature. Curry seasoning can be stored at room temperature for up to 5 months.

INGREDIENTS

- 1 pound carrots, peeled, roughly chopped

- 2 beets, peeled, roughly chopped

- 6 cups water

- 2 tbsp sea salt

- ¼ cup avocado oil

- 5 basil leaves, fresh

- 1 red onion, diced

- 3 garlic cloves, diced

- ½ tbsp oregano, dried

- 1 tbsp rosemary, dried

- 1 tbsp coconut sugar

- 2 tbsp white balsamic vinegar

- 1 cup water

"TOMATO" SAUCE

| SERVING SIZE 4 CUPS | TIME 1 HOUR |

DIRECTIONS

1. Place the 6 cups of water and sea salt in a large pot on the stove, covered, over high heat. Bring to a boil, about 10 minutes.

2. Place carrots and beets into the boiling water and cook until fork-tender, about 20–30 minutes.

3. While carrots and beets are cooking, place a large cast-iron pan on the stove over medium heat. Heat until warm, about 3 minutes.

4. Place the avocado oil and onions in the warmed cast-iron pan. Cook over medium heat until onions are translucent, stirring occasionally with a wooden spoon, about 4 minutes.

5. Add the garlic to the cast-iron pan. Continue cooking until garlic is golden brown, stirring occasionally with a wooden spoon, about 3 minutes.

6. Remove carrots and beets from the boiling water and place in a blender with 1 cup of the water from the pot. Blend until smooth, about 3 minutes.

7. Add the blended carrots and beets and the remaining ingredients to the cast-iron pan.

8. Bring the mixture to a boil, and then reduce heat and allow mixture to simmer for 25 minutes.

9. Serve warm.

STORAGE

REFRIGERATOR "Tomato" sauce can be stored in the refrigerator for up to 3 weeks.

FREEZER "Tomato" sauce can be stored in the freezer for up to 4 months.

REHEATING INSTRUCTIONS

REFRIGERATOR Place "tomato" sauce in a medium-sized pot. Place the pot on the stove over medium-low heat. Heat until warm, about 4 minutes.

FREEZER Place "tomato" sauce in a medium-sized pot. Place the pot on the stove over medium-low heat. Heat until warm, about 10 minutes.

SIDES

Caramelized Onions 154

Biscuits 156

Coconut Mozzarella 159

Mashed "Potatoes" 160

Pasta 162

"Potato" Salad 165

Roasted Garlic 167

Sweet Potato Fries 169

Flatbread Pizza 171

CARAMELIZED ONIONS

SERVING SIZE ½ CUPS   TIME 15 MINUTES

INGREDIENTS

- 4 yellow onions, sliced thinly

- ¼ cup avocado oil

- 1 tsp sea salt

DIRECTIONS

1. Place a large cast-iron pan on the stove over medium heat. Heat until warm, about 3 minutes.

2. Add the onions, avocado oil, and sea salt to the warmed cast-iron pan. Cook over medium-low heat, stirring occasionally with a wooden spoon until onions become soft and golden brown.

3. Serve warm over meat, vegetables, or seafood.

STORAGE

REFRIGERATOR Caramelized onions can be stored in the refrigerator for up to 2 weeks.

FREEZER Caramelized onions can be stored in the freezer for up to 2 months.

REHEATING INSTRUCTIONS

REFRIGERATOR Place caramelized onions in a medium-sized pot. Place the pot on the stove over medium-low heat. Heat until warm, about 2 minutes.

FREEZER Place caramelized onions in a medium-sized pot. Place the pot on the stove over medium-low heat. Heat until warm, about 7 minutes.

BISCUITS

SERVING SIZE 10 SMALL OR 5 LARGE BISCUITS   TIME 45 MINUTES

INGREDIENTS

- 1½ cup cassava flour

- 1 tbsp white balsamic vinegar

- 4 tsp baking powder

- ½ tsp sea salt

- ½ cup palm shortening, room temperature

- 1 cup coconut milk, from a can

- ¼ cup chives, fresh, diced (for savory dishes, optional)

- additional cassava flour, as needed

DIRECTIONS

1. Heat oven to 450°F. Prepare 2 baking trays by lining them each with a sheet of parchment paper.

2. In a small bowl, using a whisk, whisk the white balsamic vinegar and coconut milk together, about 10 seconds. This will make a buttermilk.

3. Place cassava flour, baking powder, chives, and sea salt in a mixing bowl. Using the whisk attachment, mix ingredients together on low speed until evenly dispersed, about 2 minutes.

4. Add palm shortening to the mixing bowl. Using the paddle attachment, mix the ingredients together until the palm shortening is coated in the dry ingredients and has broken down into smaller pieces. The palm shortening does not need to be fully incorporated into the flour; small pieces of shortening are desirable.

5. Add the white balsamic vinegar and coconut milk mixture to the mixing bowl. Using a paddle attachment, mix the ingredients together until a dough forms, about 3 minutes.

6. Dust a countertop with the additional cassava flour. Place dough onto the floured countertop. Dust the top of the dough with additional cassava flour to avoid the rolling pin from sticking to the dough. Repeat this step as needed while rolling out dough.

7. Using a rolling pin, roll out dough until it is 1 inch thick.

8. Using a rounded cookie cutter, cut dough into circles. Dough can be cut with small or large circles depending on desired size. If dough is sticking to the cookie cutter, dust the cookie cutter with additional cassava flour.

   *Coconut milk will solidify in the freezer and refrigerator, so do not worry if you see a thick layer of white after storage. It will remelt and liquify once reheated.

9. Place biscuits on the prepared baking trays.

10. Bake in the oven until tops are a light golden color, about 15 minutes for smaller biscuits and 20 minutes for larger biscuits.

11. Serve warm or at room temperature.

STORAGE

ROOM TEMPERATURE Biscuits can be stored in a covered container at room temperature for up to 3 days.

FREEZER Biscuits can be stored in the freezer for up to 2 months.

REHEATING INSTRUCTIONS

ROOM TEMPERATURE Heat oven to 325°F. Prepare 2 baking trays by lining both with a sheet of parchment paper. Heat biscuits in oven until warm, about 2–4 minutes.

FREEZER Heat oven to 350°F. Prepare 2 baking trays by lining both with a sheet of parchment paper. Heat biscuits in oven until warm, about 7–10 minutes.

INGREDIENTS

- 2 cups coconut milk, from a can

- 2 packets (7 g) gelatin

- coconut oil spray

COCONUT MOZZARELLA

SERVING SIZE 1 LOG OF MOZZARELLA   TIME 5 HOURS

DIRECTIONS

1. Prepare the mozzarella mold by taking a large drinking mug and lightly spraying the interior of the mug with coconut oil spray. This will ensure that the mozzarella does not stick to the mug.

2. Place the coconut milk in a medium-sized pot on the stove over low heat until the coconut fat has fully melted into the milk, about 3 minutes.

3. Add the gelatin to the pot, and using a whisk, whisk vigorously to incorporate into the coconut milk, about 1 minute. Turn the heat on the stove up to high and continue whisking until the coconut milk comes to a boil, about 4 minutes.

4. Remove the pot from the heat and pour the coconut and gelatin mixture into the prepared mug.

5. Place the mug in the refrigerator for at least 4 hours (up to overnight) so the mozzarella can solidify.

6. After resting the mozzarella in the refrigerator, run a knife along the perimeter of the mug to release the mozzarella from the mug's walls.

7. Shake the mozzarella out of the mug and onto a plate. Cut the top 3 cm of the mozzarella off, up to where the refrigerator has created a dried top.

8. Serve cold.

STORAGE

REFRIGERATOR Coconut mozzarella can be stored in the refrigerator for up to 1 month.

MASHED "POTATOES"

SERVING SIZE 6   TIME 1 HOUR

INGREDIENTS

- 10 cups water

- ¼ cup sea salt

- 1 head cauliflower, stem removed, roughly chopped

- 1 pound parsnips, peeled, roughly chopped

- 1 pound rutabaga, peeled, roughly chopped

- 3 cups mother sauce; recipe on page 136

- 4 cloves oven-roasted garlic; recipe on page 167

- 1 tbsp rosemary, dried

- 1 tbsp onion powder

- 1 tbsp garlic powder

- 1 tbsp sea salt

DIRECTIONS

1. Place the 10 cups of water and ¼ cup sea salt in a large pot on the stove over high heat. Cover the pot and bring water to a boil, about 10 minutes.

2. Add rutabaga to the boiling water and cook until fork-tender, about 30–40 minutes. Once it is fully cooked through, remove rutabaga from the water and place in a blender; do not discard the water or turn off the heat.

3. Once rutabaga has been removed from the boiling water, add the parsnips to the boiling water and cook until fork-tender, about 20 minutes. Once they are fully cooked through, remove the parsnips from the water and place them in the blender with the rutabaga; do not discard the water or turn off the heat.

4. Once the parsnips have been removed from the boiling water, add the cauliflower to the boiling water and cook until fork-tender, about 5 minutes. Once it is fully cooked through, remove cauliflower from the water. Water can now be discarded.

5. Blend rutabaga and parsnips together in the blender with 2 cups of the mother sauce until smooth, about 4 minutes. Once the mixture is smooth, remove it from the blender and place it in a large bowl.

6.   Place cauliflower and remaining mother sauce, along with the oven-roasted garlic and re-maining ingredients, in a blender. Blend until smooth, about 4 minutes.

7.   Once it is smooth, place the cauliflower mixture in the same bowl as the rutabaga and parsnip mixture. Using a whisk, whisk the mixtures together until smooth, about 3 minutes.

8.   Serve warm.

STORAGE

REFRIGERATOR Mashed "potatoes" can be stored in the refrigerator for up to 2 weeks.

FREEZER Mashed "potatoes" can be stored in the freezer for up to 2 months.

REHEATING INSTRUCTIONS

REFRIGERATOR Place mashed "potatoes" in a medium-sized pot with a drizzle of water. Place the pot on the stove over low heat. Heat until warm, about 4 minutes.

FREEZER Place mashed "potatoes" in a medium-sized pot with a drizzle of water. Place the pot on the stove over medium low heat. Heat until warm, about 10 minutes.

PASTA

SERVING SIZE 4	TIME 45 MINUTES

INGREDIENTS

- 1 cup cassava flour
- 2 tsp sea salt
- 1 tbsp coconut oil
- 2 tsp AIP-friendly egg substitute
- 2 tbsp water

- 1 cup water
- 6 cups water
- 2 tbsp coconut oil
- additional cassava flour, as needed
- additional coconut oil, as needed

DIRECTIONS

1. Place cassava flour and sea salt in a mixing bowl. Using the paddle attachment, mix ingredients together on low speed until fully incorporated, about 1 minute.

2. In a separate small bowl, using a whisk, whisk the egg substitute and 2 tbsp of water together until fully combined, about 10 seconds.

3. Add the egg substitute mixture, coconut oil, and 1 cup of water to the mixing bowl with the cassava flour and sea salt. Using the paddle attachment, mix ingredients together on low speed until a ball of dough forms.

4. Sprinkle some of the additional cassava flour onto a countertop. Place the pasta dough onto the floured countertop. Sprinkle some of the additional cassava flour onto the top of the pasta dough.

5. Using a rolling pin, gently roll out the pasta dough to about 1 cm thick.

6. Using a knife, cut strips of dough that are about 1 cm thick in diameter. These are your pieces of pasta.

7. The pasta can be cooked right away or dried overnight to make handling easier.

8. To dry pasta overnight, leave the pasta out on the counter or on a sheet tray uncovered. Pasta can then be stored in a glass jar in the pantry at room temperature for up to 2 months prior to cooking.

9. Place the 6 cups of water and 2 tbsp of coconut oil in a medium-sized pot on the stove over high heat. Bring water to a boil, about 10 minutes.

10. Gently place each piece of pasta into the boiling water individually. Cook pasta for 2 minutes in the boiling water. Gently strain off pasta from water; drizzle pasta lightly with additional coconut oil.

11. Serve warm.

STORAGE

REFRIGERATOR Pasta can be stored in the refrigerator for up to 1 week.

REHEATING INSTRUCTIONS

REFRIGERATOR Place pasta in pot with a drizzle of water on the stove over low heat. Heat until warm, about 2 minutes.

INGREDIENTS

- 2 rutabagas, peeled, cut into roughly 1-inch-thick pieces

- 6 cups water

- 4 tbsp sea salt

- ¼ cup chives, fresh, diced

- ½ cup white balsamic vinegar

- 1 tsp dill, fresh, chopped

- 1 tsp onion powder

- 1 tsp garlic powder

- 1 tsp coconut sugar

"POTATO" SALAD

SERVING SIZE 4	TIME 55 MINUTES

DIRECTIONS

1. Place water and salt in a large pot on the stove over high heat. Bring water to a boil, about 10 minutes.

2. Add rutabaga to boiling water and cook until fork-tender, about 40 minutes.

3. Remove rutabaga from the water and place in a large bowl.

4. Add chives, vinegar, dill, onion powder, garlic powder, and coconut sugar to the rutabaga. Toss with a spoon until evenly coated.

5. Allow mixture to cool at room temperature.

6. Serve cold.

STORAGE

REFRIGERATOR "Potato" salad can be stored in the refrigerator for up to 1 week.

INGREDIENTS

- 1 garlic head
- 1 tbsp avocado oil
- ½ tsp sea salt

ROASTED GARLIC

DIRECTIONS

1. Heat oven to 350°F. Prepare a baking tray by lining it with a sheet of parchment paper.

2. Place the garlic head, with the skin still on, on the prepared baking tray.

3. Drizzle the garlic head with the avocado oil, then sprinkle the top of the garlic head with the sea salt.

4. Place the sheet tray in the oven, bake for 30 minutes or until the garlic head turns soft and the inside is golden brown.

5. Let cool completely. Then remove the skin from the garlic cloves.

6. Serve warm over meat, fish, or vegetables. Roasted garlic cloves are very flavorful, so they should be used sparingly.

STORAGE

REFRIGERATOR Roasted garlic can be stored in the refrigerator for up to 2 weeks.

REHEATING INSTRUCTIONS

REFRIGERATOR Roasted garlic is best warmed by placing over warm meat, fish, or vegetables.

INGREDIENTS

- 1 pound sweet potatoes, peeled, cut into ¼-inch-wide strips

- 1 tbsp sea salt

- 1 tsp onion powder

- 1 tsp garlic powder

- sprinkle cinnamon, ground

- 1 tsp avocado oil

- coconut oil spray

SWEET POTATO FRIES

| SERVING SIZE 4 | TIME 45 MINUTES |

DIRECTIONS

1. Heat oven to 450°F. Prepare a sheet tray by lining it with parchment paper.

2. Toss the sweet potatoes in a bowl with the spices and coconut oil until sweet potatoes are fully coated with spices, about 1 minute.

3. Place fries on the prepared baking tray. Spray the tops of the fries lightly with coconut oil spray.

4. Bake in the oven until the fries are fork-tender and edges are golden brown, about 10–20 minutes. Spray fries lightly with coconut oil for a second time.

5. Serve warm.

STORAGE

REFRIGERATOR Sweet potato fries can be stored in the refrigerator for up to 1 week.

FREEZER Sweet potato fries can be stored in the freezer for up to 3 months.

REHEATING INSTRUCTIONS

REFRIGERATOR Preheat oven to 350°F. Prepare a sheet tray by lining it with parchment paper. Place sweet potato fries on the prepared baking tray and bake until warm, about 5–7 minutes

FREEZER Preheat oven to 350°F. Prepare a sheet tray by lining it with parchment paper. Place sweet potato fries on the prepared baking tray and bake until warm, about 10–15 minutes.

INGREDIENTS

- ½ cup cassava flour

- 1 tbsp baking powder

- ½ tsp sea salt

- 1 ⅓ cups coconut milk

- 2 tbsp avocado oil

OPTIONAL TOPPINGS

- 1 cup "tomato" sauce; recipe on page 151

- ¼ cup caramelized onions; recipe on page 154

- 1 cup sautéed chicken breast, chopped into bite sized pieces; recipe on page 57

- 6 slices coconut mozzarella; recipe on page 159

FLATBREAD PIZZA

SERVING SIZE 4   TIME I HOUR

DIRECTIONS

1.   Heat oven to 375°F. Prepare 2 baking trays by lining both with 1 sheet of parchment paper.

2.   To make the pizza dough:

   A.   Place the cassava flour, salt, and baking powder in the bowl of a mixer.

   B.   Using a paddle attachment, mix on low speed until ingredients are evenly dispersed, about 1 minute.

   C.   Pour the coconut milk and avocado oil into the mix. Using a paddle attachment, mix on medium speed until a dough forms, about 2 minutes. The dough will be very wet and crumbly.

3.   Divide dough into 2 equal portions. Place each portion of dough onto a prepared baking tray; using your hands, press each portion of dough into a circle. Press each circle of dough flat until the crust is about 2 cm thick.

4.   Place each baking tray in the oven; bake in the oven until the dough's crust expands and is a light tan color with slightly golden-brown edges, about 10–15 minutes.

5.   Remove baking trays from the oven. Spread "tomato" sauce onto flatbread pizza crusts. Top "tomato" sauce with caramelized onions and sautéed chicken breast.

6.   Once the flatbread pizzas have their toppings, place baking trays back in the oven and cook the flatbread pizzas until toppings are hot, about 10–15 minutes.

7.   Remove baking trays from the oven; allow the flatbread pizzas to cool for 5–10 minutes. Top the flatbread pizzas with the slices of coconut mozzarella. The coconut mozzarella will initially melt but will solidify after a minute or two.

8.   Cut flatbread pizzas into slices. Serve warm.

STORAGE

Flatbread pizzas are best served immediately after cooking.

DESSERT

Apple Juice Ice Pops 175

Berry Peach Cobbler 177

Brûléed Bananas 178

Cake Frosting 179

Chai Latte 181

Chocolate Chip Cookies 183

Chocolate Pudding 185

Cinnamon Apples 187

Crepes 189

Edible Chocolate Chip Cookie Dough 191

Eggnog 193

Frozen Strawberry Banana Yogurt 194

Maple Vanilla Frosting 195

Coconut Panna Cotta 197

INGREDIENTS

- 1 gal. apple juice, not from concentrate, unsweetened

- ice pop bags or ice pop molds

APPLE JUICE ICE POPS

SERVING SIZE 12   TIME 5 MINUTES

DIRECTIONS

1.   Pour apple juice into ice pop bags or ice pop molds.

2.   Place bags or molds in the freezer and freeze until juice has turned solid, about 2–3 hours depending on freezer strength.

3.   Keep in freezer until ready to serve.

4.   Serve frozen.

STORAGE

FREEZER Ice pops can be kept in the freezer for up to 6 months.

INGREDIENTS

BISCUIT DOUGH

- 1½ cups cassava flour

- 4 tbsp chives, diced

- 1 tbsp white balsamic vinegar

- 4 tsp baking powder

- ½ tsp sea salt

- ½ cup palm shortening, room temperature

- 1 cup + 1 tbsp coconut milk, from a can

- 1 tbsp coconut sugar

FRUIT FILLING

- 1 pint raspberries

- 1 pint blueberries

- 1 pint black berries

- 3 peaches, peeled, sliced thick

- 2 tbsp coconut sugar

- sprinkle sea salt

- 1 tsp vanilla extract

OTHER INGREDIENTS

- ¼ cup coconut milk, from a can

- 2 tbsp coconut sugar

- coconut oil spray

BERRY PEACH COBBLER

SERVING SIZE 4   TIME 45 MINUTES

DIRECTIONS

1. Heat oven to 375°F.

2. To make biscuit dough, place coconut milk and vinegar into a small bowl. Using a whisk, whisk vinegar and coconut milk together until combined, about 2 minutes.

3. Place the cassava flour, baking powder, chives, and salt into a mixing bowl. Using the paddle attachment, mix ingredients together on low speed until evenly dispersed, about 2 minutes.

4. Add the shortening to the flour mixture and mix using the paddle attachment on medium speed until shortening is broken up into smaller pieces, about 2 minutes.

5. Add the coconut milk and vinegar mixture into the mixing bowl and mix with the paddle attachment on medium speed until a dough forms, about 3 minutes.

6. To create the fruit filing, place all ingredients into a large bowl and toss with a spoon until all ingredients are evenly dispersed, about 1 minute.

7. To assemble cobbler, prepare a deep baking dish by lightly spraying the bottom and sides with the coconut oil spray.

8. Pour the fruit filling into the baking dish.

9. Create small biscuit dough disks by scooping teaspoon-sized balls of the biscuit dough with a spoon, then flatten the dough balls slightly with your hands. Place the biscuit dough disks onto the fruit filling in the baking dish.

10. Brush the biscuit dough disks with coconut milk and sprinkle with 1 tbsp coconut sugar.

11. Place in the oven and bake until the biscuit disks are light golden brown in color, about 20 minutes.

12. Serve warm.

STORAGE

REFRIGERATOR Berry peach cobbler can be stored in a sealed glass container for up to 1 week.

BRÛLÉED BANANAS

SERVING SIZE 4   TIME 15 MINUTES

INGREDIENTS

- 2 bananas, peeled, sliced down the middle

- 6 tbsp coconut sugar

DIRECTIONS

1. Sprinkle 1½ tbsp of coconut sugar on one side of each banana slice.

2. Using a kitchen-safe blowtorch, torch the coconut sugar on top of the banana slice until the sugar has caramelized, about 1 minute. To ensure all sugar is caramelized evenly, move blowtorch slowly across the banana slice while caramelizing sugar.

3. Serve warm.

IF YOU DO NOT HAVE A BLOWTORCH

1. Preheat oven to high broil setting.

2. Prepare a baking tray by lining it with 1 sheet of parchment paper.

3. Place the sugar-topped banana slices sugar side up on the prepared baking tray.

4. Place in the oven for about a minute or until the coconut sugar has become golden brown and caramelized.

5. Serve warm.

STORAGE

Brûléed bananas are best served immediately after baking.

CAKE FROSTING

SERVING SIZE 2 CUPS   TIME 20 MINUTES

INGREDIENTS

- 1 cup palm shortening, room temperature

- 2 tbsp coconut cream

- ¼ cup tapioca flour or tapioca starch

- ¼ cup maple syrup

- pinch sea salt

- 1 tsp vanilla extract

DIRECTIONS

1. Place the palm shortening, maple syrup, sea salt, and coconut cream in a mixing bowl. Using a paddle attachment, mix ingredients on low speed until smooth, about 5 minutes.

2. Add in tapioca flour or tapioca starch and vanilla extract to the mixing bowl. Using a paddle attachment, mix on low speed until smooth, scraping down the sides of the bowl with a spatula to ensure all ingredients are incorporated, about 4 minutes.

STORAGE

REFRIGERATOR Cake frosting can be kept in the refrigerator for up to 3 weeks.

REHEATING INSTRUCTIONS

REFRIGERATOR Cake frosting will become solid in the refrigerator. To soften, allow the frosting to sit out at room temperature for 1 hour. Place the frosting in a mixing bowl. Using a whip attachment, whisk the frosting on high speed until smooth and fluffy, about 7 minutes.

INGREDIENTS

- 3 cups coconut milk, from a can

- ⅛ tsp nutmeg, dried, ground

- ½ tsp ginger, dried, ground

- ⅛ tsp cloves, dried, ground

- ⅛ tsp allspice, dried, ground

- 1 tsp cinnamon, dried, ground

- ⅛ tsp cardamom, dried, ground

- ½ cup coconut sugar

- 2 pinches sea salt

CHAI LATTE

SERVING SIZE 2   TIME 10 MINUTES

DIRECTIONS

1. Combine all ingredients in a pot.

2. Using a whisk, whisk until spices and sugar are evenly dispersed in the coconut milk, about 2 minutes.

3. Place pot over high heat on the stove and bring to a boil. Once mixture is boiling, turn off heat and remove pot from heat.

4. Using a whisk, whisk mixture together right before serving to ensure spices are evenly dispersed, about 10 seconds.

5. Portion mixture into 2 mugs.

6. Serve warm.

STORAGE

REFRIGERATOR Mixture can be stored in refrigerator for up to 1 week.

FREEZER Mixture can be stored in freezer for up to 1 month.

REHEATING INSTRUCTIONS

REFRIGERATOR Place mixture in a pot. Place pot over medium heat on the stove, and using a whisk, whisk constantly until mixture comes to a simmer, about 5 minutes. Once mixture is warm, remove from heat and serve warm.

FREEZER Place mixture in a pot. Place pot over medium heat on the stove, and using a whisk, whisk constantly until mixture comes to a simmer, about 10 minutes. Once mixture is warm, remove from heat and serve warm.

INGREDIENTS

- ½ cup palm shortening

- 1 cup coconut sugar

- 4 tsp AIP-friendly egg substitute + 4 tbsp water

- 1 tsp vanilla

- 1¼ cup tigernut flour

- ¼ cup tapioca flour

- ½ cup cassava flour

- 2 tsp baking powder

- ⅛ tsp sea salt

- 1 cup AIP-friendly chocolate chips

STORAGE

ROOM TEMPERATURE Cookies can be kept in a sealed container at room temperature for up to 1 week.

FREEZER Cookies can be kept in the freezer for up to 3 months.

REHEATING INSTRUCTIONS

FREEZER Preheat oven to 350°F. Prepared a baking tray by lining it with 1 sheet of parchment paper. Place the cookies on the prepared baking tray. Place the baking tray in the oven and bake until cookies are warm, about 3 minutes.

CHOCOLATE CHIP COOKIES

SERVING SIZE 6 LARGE COOKIES OR 12 SMALL COOKIES   TIME 25 MINUTES

DIRECTIONS

1. Preheat oven to 350°F.

2. Prepare a baking tray by lining it with 1 sheet of parchment paper.

3. Place the palm shortening and coconut sugar in a mixing bowl. Using the paddle attachment, mix the shortening and sugar together on medium-high speed until shortening and sugar have become a smooth and fluffy mixture, about 5 minutes.

4. While shortening and sugar are mixing, in a separate bowl, whisk together the egg substitute and water with a fork or whisk until smooth, about 1 minute.

5. Add the egg substitute mixture, vanilla, and sea salt to the shortening and sugar mixture. Using the paddle attachment, mix ingredients together on medium speed until liquid has been fully incorporated, about 5 minutes.

6. Scrape down the sides of the mixing bowl with a spatula and add in the tigernut flour, tapioca flour, cassava flour, and baking powder. Using the paddle attachment, mix together on medium-low speed until a smooth dough has formed, about 3 minutes.

7. Scrape down the sides of the mixing bowl with a spatula and add in the chocolate chips. Using the paddle attachment, mix on low speed until chocolate chips are fully incorporated, about 2 minutes.

8. Scoop cookie dough into large or small balls of dough, depending on your preference.

9. Gently flatten the cookie dough balls using your hands, then place the flattened cookie dough balls onto the prepared baking tray.

10. Place the baking tray in the oven and bake until cookies are golden brown, about 10 minutes.

11. Serve warm or cooled.

INGREDIENTS

- 2 avocados, skin and pit removed
- ¼ cup carob powder
- ½ cup honey, raw
- 1 tsp vanilla extract
- 7 tbsp water

CHOCOLATE PUDDING

SERVING SIZE 2   TIME 15 MINUTES

DIRECTIONS

1.   Place all ingredients in a blender. Blend until smooth, about 6 minutes.

2.   Using a spatula, press pudding through a fine mesh sieve to obtain a very smooth texture.

3.   Serve chilled.

STORAGE

REFRIGERATOR Chocolate pudding can be stored in a sealed container for up to 1 week in the refrigerator.

INGREDIENTS

- 4 apples, any variety, peeled, sliced into ½-inch-thick slices

- ¼ cup coconut sugar

- ½ tsp cinnamon, ground

- pinch sea salt

- 2 tbsp water

CINNAMON APPLES

DIRECTIONS

1.   Heat a cast-iron pan until warm over medium heat, about 3 minutes.

2.   Add the apples, coconut sugar, and sea salt to the warmed cast-iron pan. Stir the apples with a wooden spoon until the apples are fully coated in the sugar and sea salt.

3.   Cook mixture over medium heat until apples have a golden brown color around their edges, about 5 minutes.

4.   Add the cinnamon and water to the apple mixture, stirring with a wooden spoon to combine. Cook apple mixture over low heat until apples are soft, about 5 minutes.

5.   Turn off heat, then remove pan from heat.

6.   Serve warm.

STORAGE

REFRIGERATOR Cinnamon apples can be stored in the refrigerator for up to 1 week.

FREEZER Cinnamon apples can be stored in the freezer for up to 4 months.

REHEATING INSTRUCTIONS

REFRIGERATOR Place 1 cup of cinnamon apples in a pot with 2 tbsp of water. Place the pot over medium-low heat on the stove and heat until warm, about 4 minutes.

FREEZER Place 1 cup of cinnamon apples in a pot with 2 tbsp of water. Place the pot over medium-low heat on the stove and heat until warm, about 10 minutes.

INGREDIENTS

- 2 tbsp AIP egg substitute
- 3 tbsp water
- 4 tbsp coconut oil, melted
- 1 tsp honey
- ½ tsp sea salt
- ½ cup cassava flour
- 2 cup coconut milk, from a can
- ¼ cup tigernut flour
- 1 tbsp + 1 tsp tapioca flour or tapioca starch

CREPES

SERVING SIZE 12 SMALL CREPES   TIME 40 MINUTES

DIRECTIONS

1. To make crepe batter, place the egg substitute and water into a small bowl. Using a whisk or a fork, whisk the egg substitute and water together until smooth, about 30 seconds.

2. Add the coconut oil, honey, salt, and coconut milk to the bowl. Using a whisk, whisk together until smooth, about 1 minute.

3. Add the cassava flour, tigernut flour, and tapioca flour or tapioca starch to the bowl. Using a whisk, whisk together until smooth, about 2 minutes.

4. Once crepe batter is made, heat a crepe pan or a nonstick pan on the stove over medium heat until warm, about 4 minutes.

5. Add 2 tbsp crepe batter to the warm pan. Quickly spray the back of a metal spoon with coconut oil and gently spread the crepe batter until the batter thins out to a thin layer on the pan.

6. Cook the crepe for 2 minutes, then carefully flip the crepe over to cook the other side. Cook the crepe for 1 minute, then gently remove the crepe from the pan.

7. Repeat steps 5 and 6 until all the crepe batter has been cooked.

8. Serve warm.

    Optional: Fill crepes with your favorite fillings, such as AIP-friendly chocolate chips, strawberries, and tigernut butter.

STORAGE

FREEZER Crepes can be stored in the freezer for up to 2 months. Placing a small sheet of parchment paper in between crepes in the freezer will help prevent crepes from sticking to one another.

REHEATING INSTRUCTIONS

FREEZER Heat oven to 350°F. Prepare a baking tray by lining it with parchment paper. Place crepes down on the prepared baking tray and bake in the oven until warm, about 3–5 minutes.

INGREDIENTS

- ½ cup palm shortening

- 1 cup coconut sugar

- 1 tsp vanilla extract

- 1½ cup tigernut flour

- ½ cup cassava flour

- ⅛ tsp sea salt

- 1 cup AIP-friendly chocolate chips

EDIBLE CHOCOLATE CHIP COOKIE DOUGH

SERVING SIZE 6   TIME 10 MINUTES

DIRECTIONS

1. Preheat oven to 350°F.

2. Prepare a baking tray by lining it with 1 sheet of parchment paper.

3. Place the palm shortening and coconut sugar in a mixing bowl. Using a paddle attachment, mix the shortening and sugar together on medium speed until they have become smooth and fluffy, about 5 minutes.

4. Scrape down the sides of the mixing bowl with a spatula. Add in the tigernut flour and cassava flour to the mixing bowl. Using a paddle attachment, mix ingredients together on medium-low speed until a smooth dough has formed, about 3 minutes.

5. Scrape down the sides of the mixing bowl with a spatula. Add the chocolate chips to the mixing bowl. Using a paddle attachment, mix ingredients on low speed until chocolate chips are fully incorporated, about 2 minutes.

6. Serve chilled.

STORAGE

REFRIGERATOR Edible cookie dough can be kept in the refrigerator for up to 2 weeks.

FREEZER Edible cookie dough can be kept in the freezer for up to 4 months.

REHEATING INSTRUCTIONS

FREEZER Allow edible cookie dough to come to room temperature by thawing at room temperature for about 2 hours.

INGREDIENTS

- 6 cups coconut milk, from a can

- ¼ cup coconut sugar

- 2 cinnamon sticks

- 1 tsp cinnamon, ground

- ⅛ tsp nutmeg, ground

- 2 cloves, whole

- ½ tsp ginger powder

- pinch sea salt

EGGNOG

SERVING SIZE 4   TIME 15 MINUTES

DIRECTIONS

1. Place all ingredients in a pot. Place pot over high heat on the stove; bring mixture to a boil. As mixture is coming to a boil, whisk constantly with a whisk to ensure spices become evenly dispersed.

2. Once mixture comes to a boil, lower the stove to low heat and allow mixture to simmer for 10 minutes, stirring occasionally with a wooden spoon.

3. Portion into 4 mugs or glasses.

4. Serve warm.

STORAGE

REFRIGERATOR Mixture can be stored in refrigerator for up to 1 week.

FREEZER Mixture can be stored in freezer for up to 1 month.

REHEATING INSTRUCTIONS

REFRIGERATOR Place mixture in a pot. Place pot over medium heat on the stove, and using a whisk, whisk constantly until mixture comes to a simmer, about 5 minutes. Once mixture is warm, remove from heat and serve warm.

FREEZER Place mixture in a pot. Place pot over medium heat on the stove, and using a whisk, whisk constantly until mixture comes to a simmer, about 10 minutes. Once mixture is warm, remove from heat and serve warm.

FROZEN STRAWBERRY BANANA YOGURT

SERVING SIZE 4   TIME 10 MINUTES

INGREDIENTS

- 2 bananas, sliced thin, slices frozen for at least 24 hours

- 1 cup strawberries, tops trimmed off, strawberries frozen for at least 24 hours

- 2 tbsp AIP-friendly coconut yogurt

DIRECTIONS

1. Place all ingredients in a blender. Blend until smooth, about 3 minutes.

2. Serve immediately.

STORAGE

FREEZER Frozen yogurt can be kept in the freezer for up to 1 month.

MAPLE VANILLA FROSTING

SERVING SIZE 4 CUPS   TIME 15 MINUTES

INGREDIENTS

- 1 cup palm shortening
- 1 tbsp coconut cream
- ¼ cup tapioca flour/starch
- ⅓ cup coconut sugar
- ¾ cup maple syrup
- ⅛ tsp sea salt
- 1 tsp vanilla extract

DIRECTIONS

1. Place the palm shortening and coconut sugar in a mixing bowl. Using a paddle attachment, mix palm shortening ad coconut sugar on high speed until fully smooth, about 5 minutes.

2. Using a spatula, scrape down the sides of the mixing bowl. Add the maple syrup, sea salt, vanilla extract, and coconut cream to the mixing bowl. Using a paddle attachment, mix ingredients on medium speed until smooth, about 10 minutes.

3. Using a spatula, scrape down the sides of the mixing bowl. Add in the tapioca flour or tapioca starch to the mixing bowl. Using a paddle attachment, mix ingredients until smooth, about 5 minutes.

4. Using a whip attachment, whip frosting on high speed until fluffy, about 3 minutes.

STORAGE

REFRIGERATOR Maple frosting can be kept in the refrigerator for up to 3 weeks.

REHEATING INSTRUCTIONS

REFRIGERATOR Maple frosting will become solid in the refrigerator. To soften, allow frosting to sit out at room temperature for 1 hour. Place frosting in a mixing bowl. Using a whip attachment, whisk frosting on high speed until smooth and fluffy, about 7 minutes.

INGREDIENTS

- 3 cups coconut milk, from a can

- 3 tbsp coconut sugar

- 1 tsp vanilla extract

- 2 tsp AIP-friendly gelatin

- 1 tbsp water

- coconut oil spray